DIARY
OF A
PASTOR'S
WIFE

Lady Eleanor L. Williams

www.eleanorwilliams.com

Published by:
Majestic Priesthood Publication, Freeport, Grand
Bahama, Bahamas.
Email: mpppublications@gmail.com

1-242-727-2137

Printed in the United States of America

DIARY
OF A
PASTOR'S
WIFE

To Sandra,

May this Diary
be a blessing
in Your life!

[signature]

CONTENTS

FOREWORD

THIS BOOK WILL ABSOLUTELY empower every woman that reads it with wisdom to support themselves, their husbands, family and the church in the things of God! I have known Eleanor Williams for many years and she lives what she preaches, which is of utmost importance. She submits to her husband and works closely with him in family, ministry and business. The wealth of knowledge of this principled woman of God has been carefully communicated. As a result, this book promises to be filled with insights to transform your life. I highly recommend this book!

Dr. Kelabo Z. Collie, M.D.

DEDICATION

THIS BOOK IS DEDICATED to all pastors' wives, including those who desire to be a pastor's wife. To my dearly beloved departed mother, my first mentor and coach, Clotilda Wilson Ferguson, who was also a pastor's wife.

PREFACE

A PASTOR'S WIFE: LIKE PARENTING, there is no manual that outlines the step to becoming the ideal women in the role.

Pastors' wives are the women who undergird the saints; they are the wind beneath the wings of their husband and his ministry, an earthly shield and personal prayer intercessor. They are the "Most Valuable Player (M.V.P.)" in the pews, but many pastors' wives were never told so, or given any opportunity or outlet to express themselves publically.

These women are "the mid-wives" of the Church, standing in the gap by faith, as a stronghold and fortitude for the congregation. Behind the scenes with broad shoulders, a pastor's wife helps carry her husband, helping him to stand tall and strong during many trials and tribulations.

Despite their faithfulness, the wives of many pastors have died in silence, with unspoken requests, or heart's desires not being honored or fulfilled. These women sometimes stand in the shadows of ministry, but are actually steadfast, powerful prayer warriors. These women wake up at the crack of dawn, when all is still and quiet to present the needs of the church before the Lord. God hears her cries, and like a mother giving birth, she travails for the ministry in the spiritual realm through fervent prayer — a pregnant woman giving birth to all that is new, and setting the standard of holiness for others to follow. However, in ministry, on numerous occasions, pastors' wives are like roses that get pierced repeatedly in a garden among thorns.

In previous times, the pastor's wife was referred to as the "mother of the church." Today, they are known as "first ladies," only to be known — it seems —for occupying the front pew with big hats and lace handkerchiefs. Yet, like the oil from an alabaster box, she gives perfume to things called dead, and ointment to those that are wounded.

I thank God for my beloved, belated mother, Clotilda A. Wilson-Ferguson, who was a pastor's wife for more than forty years. By example, she taught me what it means to display a meek and quiet spirit, and also how to live an exemplary life that reflects that of the Proverbs 31 woman. She taught me how to be a pastor's wife. And this book will help you bring out the best in you as a pastor's wife in such a way you will feel fulfilled supporting your husband and the ministry or church.

Our Pastors' Wives

When we thank God for our Pastor,
We must give Him thanks for two,
For when your husband came to us
God also sent us to you.

A pastor's wife must be many things,
You have many hats to wear;
And we say thanks for all you do
And lift you up in prayer.

You adjust your life to meet the needs
Of your husband's congregation,
And it seems that you can always cope
With almost any situation.

Your presence blesses all of us
Who know you from day to day?
As our pastor's wife, you are serving God
In a fine and worthy way.

— **Helen Bush**

ACKNOWLEDGEMENTS

In writing this book, I give glory, honor and all praise to God, our Heavenly Father and to the Holy Spirit for giving me the intuition, patience, grace, wisdom and resources to write this book during this season of my life.

I salute all pastors' wives reading this diary. Special thanks is given to Pastor's wives in Freeport, Grand Bahama, Bahamas where my husband and I are pastors. Thanks to my ninety-five -year-old father, Bishop Cephas Ferguson, who was my first pastor during my childhood and adolescent years; special thanks is also given to my father-in-law, the late Bishop Arnold F. Williams, who was the pastor that began to push me into my purpose and destiny.

Warmest and exceptional thanks is given to my current pastor and phenomenal husband, Bishop Patterson A. Williams; thank you for your unwavering encouragement, wisdom, support and love.

My warmest sentiments go out to our two sons, Eleason and Ele'leon Williams; I love you, and you both are special gifts from God — you are our two masterpieces.

To Dr. Deryl G. Hunt and Mrs. Hunt, thank you for your legacy and awesome spiritual impartation. To my five sisters and two brothers, thank you for your unwavering love and encouragement. To Avril Mitchell and Benita Pinder, thank you for the role you both played. Last, but not least, to my church family, Church of Christ Apostolic, a non-denominational ministry with warmest love — a thousand thanks!

ABOUT THE AUTHOR

ELEANOR LOUISE FERGUSON-WILLIAMS WAS born on the seventh day, of the seventh month in 1962. She was born in Nassau, Bahamas. Her parents are Bishop Cephas Ferguson and the late Clotilda Wilson-Ferguson. Her stepmother is Minister Anamae Ferguson.

Lady Eleanor is a "pastor's kid," and the eighth of nine children —three boys and six girls. Lady Eleanor grew up in a Christian home, and accepted Jesus Christ as Savior, at the tender age of fifteen.

Lady Eleanor is a graduate of R. M. Bailey Senior High School in Nassau, New Providence, and a graduate of The Bahamas Hotel Training College. She has worked in the hospitality field for most of her adult life. Lady Eleanor also holds a Bachelor's degree in Christian Counseling from Universal Bible College Incorporated.

In October of 1987, Lady Eleanor relocated to Freeport, Bahamas, after she had met and married the one God had set aside for her — Patterson Williams — who is now her senior pastor. She has been married for over thirty years, and she is a mother of two wonderful sons: Eleason and Ele'leon.

Lady Eleanor serves with her husband in pastoring Church of Christ Apostolic, a non-denominational ministry, located at #19 Pioneers Loop, on the island of Grand Bahama, Bahamas. Lady Eleanor is a prophetic voice emerging from diversity to unity in the body of Christ. She is a community leader, motivational and conference speaker, kingdom leadership skills agent, and a Justice of the Peace in the Bahamas. Her favorite pastimes include travelling and spending quality time with her family.

Lady Eleanor's personal philosophy and favorite Bible verse is: *"I can do all things through Christ who strengthens me"* (Philippians 4:3).

PART 1

The Anatomy and Dynamics of the Role of a Pastor's Wife

—— *Chapter 1* ——

WHO IS THE PASTOR'S WIFE?

T HE PASTOR'S WIFE IS simply the wife of a pastor. This is a woman who is married to the pastor. Be who you are. The pastor's wife is an ordinary woman playing the role as her husband's helper. Beside every successful man is a great woman. It is not good for man to be alone. Before the creation of woman, man was a solitary individual. From his side, God made a woman. "*And the rib which the lord God had taken from man, made him a woman and bought her unto the man."* (Genesis 3v22)

Many churches call their pastor's wife "the first lady," some call her the "mother of the church." There are two areas in life where the term "first lady" is appropriate: when referring to the wife of a President or a Prime minister of a country, and when referring to the queen of England.

Nothing in the Bible indicates that the spouse of a Pastor should receive some sort of honorary title such as, "First Lady." Doing so elevates the pastor's wife above others; this title of "First Lady" puts undue pressure on her, and this also goes against biblical instruction for Christian women leaders, which is to serve and remain humble. It's not a sin if a local church chooses to call their pastor wife "First lady" or "Lady" which we all are. It only shows a high level of respect for her title.

The church offices listed in Ephesians 4:11–13 are apostles, prophets, evangelists, shepherds (pastors) and teachers. We are told God gave these leaders to:...*equip the saints for the work of ministry, for building up the body of Christ, until we all attain to the unity of the faith, and of the knowledge* of the Son of God, to mature manhood, to the measure of the stature of the fullness of Christ, so that we may no longer be children, tossed to and fro by the waves and carried about by every wind of doctrine, by human cunning, by craftiness in deceitful schemes.

Rather, by speaking the truth in love, we are to grow up in every way, into him who is the head, into Christ, from whom the whole body is joined and held together by every joint with which it is equipped, when each part is working properly, makes the body grow so that it builds itself up in love" (Ephesians 4:12–16).

There is no mention of the title or position of "First Lady" in the Bible. Too often we bring titles or cliques into the body of Christ that are not in the Bible, and we accept them in many of our Christian churches globally. The Bible says to call the older women "mothers." However, many pastors' wives do not want to be identified as the "mother" of the church because of their mindset about the lifestyle or duties of a mother in the natural, rather than seeing a "mother" in the spiritual sense, that is, one who is mature and experienced in spiritual things.

The pastor's wife is very special to him as his helpmeet and partner in ministry. She should be respected highly by the congregation, but when she begins to think of herself more highly than she should, that can create a challenge in her fellowship with the saints, especially the women in the ministry.

A petite, beautiful lady privately seated on her own small, "private bench," which is built for only one person, is not the true signature of a pastor's wife. A broad hat, elegant and expensive suits, nails neatly manicured, and a fan to stay cool, is not the "standard and inexorable look" of a pastor's wife. Stay true to yourself, and your own sense of style, but be sure that the manner in which you dress, or present yourself is appropriate and respectful, and glorifies God.

The pastor's wife should have a servant's heart; she should avail herself to serve the people, rather than seeking for others to serve her. 2 Corinthians 4:5 says, *"For what we proclaim is not ourselves, but Jesus Christ as Lord, with ourselves as your servants for Jesus' sake."*

You must know that always having someone carry your bag, Bible and shoes is not a sign of servanthood on your part. Having a person to be with you all the time as your armor-bearer, cleaning your home, keeping your children, taking you to and from church, shopping with you, and driving you everywhere, is actually not underpinned by biblical laws or principles. Therefore, this practice is not scriptural and should be discontinued if it is being done at your church.

Some congregations use the expression "First Lady" so casually because it has been accepted by many churches all over the world. The expression "First Lady" sounds so glamorous, so alluring, so elegant, so charming, so charismatic, but it is "so not scriptural." A pastor's wife is more than just a "First Lady;" she is "the leading lady elect." 2 John 1:1 says, "...*and one who wears many caps and has the capability to lead all women, young and old by being the right example.*" She is almost always, a reliable helper and also an under-appreciated servant.

The wife of a pastor can be hurt in a myriad of ways—through attacks on her husband, attacks on her children, and attacks on her. Her pain is magnified by one great reality: she cannot fight back, or rather, should not retaliate in the natural. The Bible says, "*For the weapons of our warfare are not carnal, but mighty through God to the pulling down of strongholds*" (2 Corinthians 10:4). She deals with the hurt in silence most of the time. It takes a bonfire Christian, to be a pastor's wife, and to handle all the pressures that come with it. And that is the problem: in most cases, she is pretty much "the same kind of Christian as everyone else." When the enemy attacks, she bleeds.

Your role as a pastor's wife can be challenging: whether it is a tired husband coming home to whom you need to show some care, or your role in dealing with the family while he travels around the world. Sometimes, there will be persons in your church who really love, respect and appreciate your husband, but will not think much of you.

I often pray for all the mighty women of God that have been called to be the wife of a pastor. You are a strong woman! You have a great call and purpose in your life. Don't give up! Let God be the source to meet every need you may have.

Esther changed the future of her people, and Ruth was obedient and showed honor. These women received blessings beyond what they could have imagined though their humility, honor and reverence for the Lord. I am so honored to be a pastor's wife that God has called to support my husband's conventional and non-conventional ministry. Together, my husband and I are helping to build God's Kingdom.

As his wife, your husband needs you to be involved in his calling by supporting him. That does not mean you should lose your identity, or that what you do outside of supporting your husband in ministry is not important. The fact that the Lord has called you to be the wife of a pastor or minister is a great honor!

----- *Chapter 2* -----

THE ROLE OF
A PASTOR'S WIFE

I N REALITY, THERE IS no one way approach on
the actual role of a pastor's wife. The wife does
not do the work of the pastor but the pastor
and his wife are a team who are yoked together
to do God's work. Few recognize the reality of
this and want to put the pastor's wife in a box
and delegate her to do some type of traditional
church work. She needs to be a prayer supporter
for her husband.

> Wives be subject to your husbands — be submissive and adapt yourselves to your own husbands as (a service) unto the lord. For the husband is head of the wife as Christ is the head of the church. Himself the head of (his) body. As the church is subject, so let wives also be subject in everything to their husband. (Ephesians 5v 22-24)

The Bible does not address the involvement of the pastor's wife in any ministry. In other words, it depends upon the denomination, the individual church within a denomination, the church board, the pastor of that church, and his wife to determine how active the pastor's wife is to support and be submissive to her husband. However, if the Lord calls a man into the ministry, He calls the whole man and that includes the man's wife and his family. The ministry is a partnership in all areas of life, not only in the home life.

Though the job of a pastor's wife can be exciting and challenging, not all women relate to it in the same way.

Three Categories of the Role of Pastors' Wives

(Which category are you?)

THE DETACHED PASTOR'S WIFE

This type of pastor's wife does not perceive herself as a particularly important part of her husband's ministry. She's married to a man, not his job. She is not concerned about her husband's work. She is not concerned about the expectation of her husband's congregation. Her main preoccupation will be on her domestic and occupational roles (career) and her children. This may affect his ministry negatively, as she wants her individuality to be maintained.

THE SUPPORTIVE PASTOR'S WIFE

The supportive pastor's wife can be more appropriately called the background supporter. She feels she is part of the ministry but prefers to work in the background. She knows her role and does a whole lot helping other saints out on committees and attending all services. She shows forth a meek and quiet spirit which in the sight of God is a great price, so that she may teach the young women to be sober, to love their husbands, and to love their children (Titus 2:4). She has a beautiful spirit but does not want to play a leading role in the church.

INCORPORATED PASTOR'S WIFE

The last category of Pastors' wives is the incorporated participant. She is actively involved in the ministry. Such a wife has in fact found her particular niche —a ministry of her own that complements that of her husband. She may teach, preach, visit or counsel when her husband is absent. This type is almost an assistant pastor, one who is always visible next to her husband. The pastor and his wife is a team who are yoked together to do God's work. Too few recognize the reality of this, and they want to put the pastor's wife in a box; they relegate her to keeping the fires burning at home, and to praying for her husband. That certainly is her responsibility, but quite often the pastor's wife has gifts that can, and should be used in the ministry.

Her role does not necessarily include leading the praise team, playing the piano or organ, being an extra worker in the church, or even being the women's ministry leader. I have heard a pastor's wife state that her role is basically the same as any other wife in the church, which is to honor, love and support her husband. On the other hand, there are women whose husbands are pastors, and they see it as "his ministry," and do not enter into the work of the ministry in anyway. There should be a good balance between these two ideas, with the goal of bringing glory to God in all things. An active, outgoing pastor's wife is a valuable asset to any church in today's climate of apathy towards the things of God.

Pastors' wives, and the role of pastors' wives, have been grossly misunderstood over the years. Many have their opinion about how they perceived a pastor's wife should conduct herself, or perform her duties, and how her role should be defined.

A pastor's wife should not necessarily be employed by the church, but she should utilize her God-given gifts to volunteer in various areas of ministry. A pastor's wife's priorities are to God first, then to her husband and children, and then to the members of the church.

It is wonderful to have an attractive "first lady" who is beautiful on the inside as well as the outside. However, the term "first lady" may have glamorous and prestigious connotations, but there is so much more that goes on in the life of pastors' wives and it is not always glamorous.

There are women who become pastors' wives after getting married. This means that their husband answered the call of God after they were married. Therefore, technically, she did not marry a pastor. However, some women marry a man who already is a pastor. Some pastors' wives are seemingly "thrown" into ministry with their husbands, while others never wanted to be pastors' wives; so, when the pressures of the ministry begin to press down, she begins to crumble under the weight. Never compare yourself to another pastor's wife.

Being seated on the front pew with fashionable outfits, with a lace handkerchief over the knees, and wearing a pearl necklace, are "a front" or a false image. Pastors' wives are women of God who should maintain their homes, jobs, husbands, children, and themselves, and still be able to function within the church. The pastor's wife does not have to be a frontline speaker, but she is called to be by her husband's side, and to take care of his needs and their children.

Many pastors' wives are powerful behind the scenes, and in being so, they make their husbands look good. I believe every pastor's wife is called of God and that she has an assignment in the ministry that is more than just being his wife, whether she accepts it or not. A lady who chooses to marry a pastor, chooses a life's work. One of the greatest challenges of pastors' wives, is that they fight against a sense of inadequacy and lack of confidence. Stop looking at yourself, for you can never be enough in yourself; but rather look to God who called you both, for He only is your sufficiency. That's the place of His grace rubbing on you to function well in the ministry.

Furthermore, one of the truly remarkable qualities of a pastor's wife is when she is able to show sincere, steadfast love for the church members she serves. I believe there is a special anointing upon a pastor's wife to go beyond the normal call of duty. It is a patient, gentle love, almost as though the person she is helping is a young child. A pastor's wife often understands that baby Christians, no matter how old, can be acting out because they are hurting.

A pastor's wife provides a sounding board for her husband to vent, brainstorm, and question his progress or goals. She is encouraging and steadfast in supporting the vision that God has given to them. She is often a nurse, healing emotional wounds that could cause a pastor to give up. She is a counselor, who helps her husband to work out difficulties that are too close for him to see entirely, or too complex for him to solve alone.

A pastor's wife is a lover and a protector who shields him from harm, and she provides the loving care that is so vitally needed, especially when he feels he is in a lonely profession. Many pastors do not have close friends who they can vent to, or share their problems with. A pastor's wife provides that companionship that encourages him to continue, even when he feels like giving up, as she is his personal cheerleader.

What great assurance a pastor has, when he has a wife who knows how to pray, and how to get a hold of God! She prays for him and his ministry. She prays for the children; she prays through a problem or a crisis. She draws her strength, not from his love alone, but from God. Her life and dedication to her husband and his ministry is established in God, and her faithfulness is first to God. This is pleasing to the Heavenly Father. In so doing, it will definitely please her husband as well. In giving, you will always receive. This is God's law of sowing and reaping, and it works in marriage as well. As a helpmeet, a pastor's wife gives of herself, and she receives love and honor in great measure.

A pastor's wife provides that companionship that encourages him to continue even when he feels like giving up. Don't be intimidated. Some wives become intimidated by other pastors' wives doing things differently. This can be very annoying and almost creates a confrontation. Be patient; it may take some time but be yourself, love the people, win them over and create change slowly.

—— Chapter 3 ——

My Experience as a Pastor's Daughter and a Pastor's Wife

"Train up a child in the way that he should go and when he is old, he will not depart from it" (Proverbs 22:6). "If you spare the rod you will spoil the child". *I was bought up on the Bible and the belt.* "He that spareth his rod hateth his son but he that loveth him chastened him betimes." (Proverbs 13v24)

I WAS MY MOTHER'S SEVENTH pregnancy. I was born on the seventh day of the seventh month, in 1962. I was the eighth child born in a family of nine children: six girls and three boys, which included a set of twins. I was given the name Eleanor Louise Ferguson. I was affectionately called "Buddy," and still, to this day, persons from my childhood and family members, call me by that name.

I grew up in a small close-knitted community where it took a village to raise a child. Everyone was able to correct you or be your parents. Our house was a small two-bedroom wooden structure. We grew up with very limited resources. We did not know what it meant to be poor or neither did we beg for food because we never went to bed hungry and my parents always gave to others.

When I was born in 1962, my father was already a pastor. We grew up in The Church of God of Prophecy. He was a man faithful to prayer. He preached under the anointing of the Holy Spirit and I saw change and transformation in the lives of many persons he prayed for. At that time, the place of worship was affectionately called the "jumper church" because the members jumped up and down a lot, while worshiping with hands clapping, drums beating, horn blowing, and much moving and dancing around under the Holy Ghost unction.

We had a very large family; nine siblings and my parents made eleven persons in the household. My father drove a large station wagon vehicle. It was a very unique car with three set of seats or sections. My parents sat in the front portion of the vehicle, along with my oldest brother. The middle seat had four of us siblings, and the back seat, which faces the oncoming traffic, held my other four siblings.

Attending church services was our "social life." We attended church on Tuesday evening for youth meeting, Wednesday for mid-week worship service, Thursday was the women's ministry night service, Saturday was our choir practice, and on Sundays, we had four services that day. The first church service on Sunday began at 10am. Sunday school was that morning, and the morning worship service would start at 11:30am. Afternoon Sunday school was at 4pm, and finally, night service was at 7:30pm. On Sundays, we wore the same clothing from morning until the end of the night service.

Night services would sometimes run late, and we would end up being there as late as 10pm if "the Holy Ghost took over the service." It is just amazing how we looked forward to attending church because it was our form of getting out of the house for fellowship, and our chance to meet up with, talk to and have fun with our friends.

Going to church in my childhood days was fun. We also had the good examples that our parents made by the way they lived; so we had no excuse to be contrary. They taught us only as much as they knew, but they meant well.

The standards and rules of the house were very strict, and our life was a perpetual cycle: home, school, church, and back home. We knew nothing else. To us, during that time, anything outside of our daily routine was maybe a sin, and had to be scrutinized very closely.

Whenever the school would send home letters pertaining to the school activities and functions, my mother would say, "Go and ask your daddy." Once he said no, that "NO" was final. So, we as children had to find a way to get out of the house, to be with our friends. We would go to school events only if it was educational.

Most of the time we would use the term "educational," when in actuality, it was used as a pawn for us to be with our friends. Most of my friends were from church, so I enjoyed going to church. My father had pastored seven parishes of Church of God of Prophecy, so it gave me an opportunity to meet many new friends.

As my father moved around and pastored churches, my mother faithfully followed him without hesitation. I have seen her faithfulness in ministry over the years. She was not actively involved in frontline church ministry, nor did she sit in the front seat with a handkerchief on her knees, like you see so many pastors' wives do today. However, I admired her for her meek, quiet, and humble spirit. Pastors' wives in times past were seen, and not heard. She basically cared for us and took care of the home. She was very faithful in her church attendance and to the ministry.

In our family of nine children, which included a set of twins, we were all only one year apart. My mother had to get a helper in the house because she and my father had a dry goods store, and the business kept them very busy.

Every adult in the community was our parent. We stayed inside as children. For the most part, we played with one another on the inside. My parents were extremely overprotective when it came to us, and they closely monitored who "come into our space."

My mother taught me so much including how important it is to be mature in the Lord. She showed me how to love people and be hospitable. My parents were always giving to others, always looking out for the poor and the less privileged. My mother taught me the importance of living an exemplary life, being blameless, not nagging or being a brawler.

As we grew and became adults, our family structure was like a monument in the church and community. Disappointingly, one of my sisters became pregnant at the tender age of sixteen, still in high school, and this bought a sense of embarrassment on our family. My father, being a senior pastor over a large congregation, thought it fit to put my sister out of our dwelling home. She lived with our grandmother until the time of her delivery. I saw my mother's love on display as she would occasionally visit and attend to my sister, showing love, forgiveness and care for her and the baby.

The responsibility of my parents was an awesome task and I think they did well despite the shortcomings. My sister now has a children and young girl's ministry and has forgiven my father for his past decision. We are all married now and taking our rightful place in ministry and the society.

In observing my parents, I have learned how to love and care for people. The people of God are not always pleasant and kind, but the one who has called you to lead, will bless you with the grace to love and serve. Dealing with different personalities can be challenging at times. You have to know when to speak and when to be quiet or just take it to the Lord in prayer. Moses said he would rather suffer with the people of God, than to enjoy the pleasures of sin for a season (Hebrews 11:25). At times, I saw my parents suffered in ministry, not as evil doers, but as unto the Lord. You must be able to endure being backbitten, slandered, insulted or disrespected.

"Thou therefore endue hardness as a good solider of Jesus Christ. No man that warreth entangled himself with the affairs of this life, that he may please him who hath chosen him to be a solider, And if a man also strive for masteries yet is he not crowned except he strive lawfully." (2 Timothy 2:3-5).

My life as a senior pastor's wife began more than twenty years ago. I'm not sure if my parents knew I was going to become a pastor's wife. My husband being a PK (Pastor's kid) helped us both in the early stages of our ministry. My husband was an ordained minister just before we got married and felt the call of God for full time pastoral ministry years later.

The Lord being our helper, we did not meet a church and congregation already built with all of the structure, elders and ministers in place. We had to plant a new church.

Church planting is a process that results in a new local church being established. Starting a new church can feel like jumping out of an airplane without a parachute if you're not called to a Pastorate ministry. It calls for much prayer, suffering, sacrifice and patience. Husband and wife must be on one accord.

It all began in the comfort of our home with my husband and our son in August of 1995. The ministry was based on much teaching and Bible study. After worshiping few years in our home, the Lord showed we should move by faith and begin to have service in a public place. The membership had much addition. We rented a room in a local hotel for Sunday mornings. Before the service, my husband and I had to clean and remove items from previous night function events to prepare for the saints' arrival.

Keep in mind we had to pick a family up on the way to service. Sunday evening services were held at the associate pastor's home who lived in a small two-bedroom rented apartment. The Spirit and presence of the Lord followed us at both locations. After much prayer and ending of another season, we then moved to a rental building with a desire to rent to own. After many years of ministry at this location, the church membership grew and the Lord intervened, as we were blessed to purchase two acres of property and to this day, the building stands on #19 Pioneers loop, Freeport, Bahamas. To God we give all praise.

We both grew up in the same denomination, so it made it easier to flow in our own ministry. Make sure you have spousal support if you have a pastoral calling. Church planting will likely take a greater toll on pastors' wives and the children than the pastor. My husband was the youth director and also evangelized in our previous church for many years. I was the women's president so we both had experience and exposure to leadership. I knew my husband would become a pastor but never knew God had it to be out of that denomination.

It's easier when everything is in place and you just come in with your family and begin to carry on with the vision and take it to the next level. We had to serve, train and minister to people all in the same season. The most challenging season in ministry is finding faithful coaches and mentors in your life.

While working full time, being a young mother and wife, I had to play the roles of a pastor's wife all at the same season. I thank God every day for my exposure and experience in my father's house, watching him and my mother dealing with family, a congregation, the home and a business. Being a pastor's wife is not a title an individual should vote for or accept by choice, but it should be taken upon as a high calling or gift given by God. This title does not come with a Manuel, one has to be given a special grace to love, serve and care for culturally different people. You must have a prayerful lifestyle and full of the Holy Ghost.

As a pastor's wife, you will watch many people come and go as you build the ministry. Some may not like your mission statement or vision the Lord assigned to you. It's like a revolving door, some go and others stay. I have learned over the years that not everyone comes to stay. Do not get attached to any family or individual. Be watchful not to find yourself in "clicks" or favoritism. The Lord has some folks to stay for only a season. Some seasons are longer than others.

As a wife, elect lady, and mother of the church, be faithful to every season.

Chapter 4

COMPLETE HIM NOT COMPETE WITH HIM

And God said let us make man in our image, after our likeness; and let them have dominion over the fish of the sea, and the fowl of the air, and over the cattle and over all the earth. So God created man in his own image, in the image of God created he him; male and female created he them *(Genesis 1:26).*

And God blessed them, and God said unto them, be fruitful and multiply, and replenish the earth, and subdue it; and have dominion over the fish of the sea, and over the fowl of the air and over every living thing that moves upon the earth *(Genesis 1:28).*

BEING FRUITFUL IS NOT only symbolic of bringing forth natural children, but bringing forth spiritual children. We all know that the female has a womb; she is the carrier, but the male has the seed. Even though she brings the baby forth, both (male and female) carry and care for the baby together. So it is also with spiritual children. The Lord will place gifts in each of us (husband and wife) that will enable spiritual children to be birthed. That spiritual seed is in both the husband and wife, and as those gifts are activated through the Holy Spirit, they can be used to help people come to know the Lord. No man or woman can say they did it, because only God can create life and draw persons nigh to Him.

The Lord has bestowed on my husband, several offices or ministries: he is the senior pastor, Bishop, an evangelist, an expert teacher, and the list goes on. However, my husband knows that the Lord has bestowed on me a prophetic voice and mantle, an anointing to lead women. We complement one another. We do not compete as to who can preach the best sermon, who can draw the largest crowd, or who has the most speaking engagements. We both represent the Kingdom of God; we both see ourselves as co-laborers with God.

Wives, never stop giving your husband compliments: "You did a great job honey!" "I was so blessed from the message today." "You look nice today." Men like compliments too!

Supporting one another with prayers, and your presence is important. It is a great feeling, comfort, and confidence-builder when I have my husband by my side during my speaking engagements. He would pray for me in the car, on the way to my speaking engagements, and assure me that his prayers are with me, and that the Lord will bless me to minister to the people. He would encourage me not to look at the faces, but to go forth and be used by God. After ministering, I look forward to his embrace letting me know how the Lord has truly anointed me to minister to the people. We should always be careful to give God all the praise and all the glory.

God called my husband to be a pastor, and God called me to be a wife to my husband. There are some who think "I have the ear of the pastor," and they try to get me to be the go-between for whatever agenda they are pushing. However, because I go to bed with him, does not mean that I am his "Holy Spirit." God has given my husband wisdom in areas others do not see.

My husband, my lover, my best friend, the one I am "doing life with," and I love him. I am also the only one that can fulfill his desires. My job is to be his helpmeet, to encourage him, and to love on him. Our marriage needs prayers. We practice praying as a couple every morning as we get up and every night before bedtime.

Your husband needs you, as his wife, to be actively involved in his calling to the ministry, and for you to support him. That does not mean you should lose your identity, or that what you do is not important. The fact that the Lord would call you to be the wife of a pastor, or a minister is a great honor!

Give your husband over to the Lord. He belongs to God, and God has called him to be a minister. I do believe that men of God need to try to balance ministry, marriage and family. However, the worst thing we can do as wives, is pull on our husbands, and distract them from doing what God has called them to do because of our neediness. Our husbands can never meet all of our needs—only God can.

The children, as well as the church, must see the wife submitting to her husband as unto the Lord (Ephesians 5:22) because this behavior will carry over into the church, or set the tone for the church. The pastor's wife can represent the church or Bride of Christ. Believers in Jesus Christ are the bride of Christ and we wait with great anticipation for the day when we will be united with our Bridegroom. Until then, we remain faithful to Him and say with all the redeemed of the Lord, *Come, Lord Jesus* (Revelation 22:20).

A pastor-husband who has his wife's respect for his God-given authority and leadership, will have the confidence to lead his family and the church. If the wife would have any position or ministry in the church, it will be as a result of her submission to her husband's leadership.

It is important to recognize that husbands were never commanded to "exercise authority over their wives!" The headship of the husband is stated as a fact, but the command to submit is always given to the wife. The husband is commanded to love his wife sacrificially. Paul tells husbands in Ephesians 5:25, "*Love your wives, just as Christ also loved the church and gave himself up for her.*" Paul also tells wives in Ephesians 5:22, "*Be subject to your own husbands as to the Lord.*" When husbands and wives each focus on their God-ordained responsibilities towards one another, there will be harmony, and not discord and abuse.

Neither one of us has authority over each other, we're more like a team. The pastor doesn't have authority over the wife with a force. He mustn't silence her while she too should not be afraid of him.

To be in authority does not in any way, imply the superiority of the husband, and the inferiority of the wife. In some cases, a wife may in fact, be superior in intellect and spiritual maturity compared to her husband. Paul affirms in Galatians 3:28 that she is just as much a member of Christ as her husband. Peter calls the wife a "fellow-heir of the grace of life" in 1 Peter 3:7 — "*Likewise ye husbands dwell with them according to knowledge giving honor unto the wife as unto the weaker vessel and as being heirs together of the grace of life, that your prayers be not hindered.*" She is in every way, equal as a person to her husband, but God has ordained the principle of authority for the orderly functioning of government, the church, and the home. To resist it, is to resist God who ordained it. We have to humble ourselves, and yield to God, and then to one another. "*Let every soul be subject to the higher powers. For there is no power but of God; the powers that be are ordained of God.*" (Romans 13:1)

—— Chapter 5 ——

ARE YOU THE PASTOR'S WIFE OR HIS KNIFE?

A gentle answer turns away wrath, but a harsh word stirs up anger. The tongue of the wise commends knowledge, but the mouth of the fool gushes folly. The eyes of the Lord are everywhere, keeping watch on the wicked and the good. (Proverbs 15:1)

M ANY WOMEN ARE CALLED to be a pastor's wife, while others are chosen. There are many ladies who desired to never be a pastor's wife. If a woman never had the desire to be the wife of a pastor, it means that the Lord has to help that woman to yield in obedience and humility, firstly to Him, then to her husband, and then unto the ministry of the church. Otherwise, she will either help or harm his ministry.

A pastor's wife should be his biggest cheerleader, his prayer partner, co-laborer, team player, and the most intimate person in his life. She should not be his female armor bearer, "the leading deaconess," or any other woman for that matter. Additionally, the wife of a pastor should never be guilty of slander towards her husband; she should always keep him covered, in prayer and consecrations. She should not be a part of "church clicks," gossip, lying or any other works of the flesh.

The wife of the pastor should see her husband, first of all, as the "priest" of her home, "the Lord's Bishop," or a man of God, before she can see him as the father of her children, her lover or her friend. She should always focus on the spiritual life of her husband — the way God created him. Also, the pastor and his wife are "brother and sister in the Lord," fearfully and wonderfully made!

Some wives speak very disrespectfully to their husbands. This behavior is unacceptable, and should never be displayed in public or private. Remember, your husband is your pastor, and the one who watches over your soul. Always respect and honor his office as one who is called by God. It is important to always be discerning, watchful and prayerful in regards to other women in the ministry, who may be planning or strategizing to come against your husband. Ask the Lord to bless you to be your husband's spiritual eyes, looking out for those "goats" in sheep's clothing. Always allow the Holy Spirit to guard you and lead you into all truth. Put on the whole armor of God every day to avoid those subtle spirits. You have to put on the whole armor of God every morning when you wake up by saying the scripture aloud: *"Put on God's whole armor, the armor of a heavy armed soldier, which God supplies that you may be able success- fully to stand up against all the strategies and the deceits of the devil. For we are not wrestling with flesh and blood – contending only with physical opponents but against the despotisms against the powers against the master spirits, who are the world rulers of this present darkness against the spirit forces of wickedness in the heavenly sphere.*

Therefore put on God's complete armor that you may be able to resist and stand your ground on the evil day and having done all to stand, still stand." (Ephesians 6:11-13)

I am God's. My first and foremost identity is found in my Savior, Jesus Christ. I am fearfully and wonderfully made with His image stamped on me! I am bought with a price far above rubies! A child of God is who I am. I bear His image, and I want to experience this life with eternity in mind. When the tug-of-war of all the roles and identities placed on my human flesh seem to overwhelm me, I want to remember whose I am, and who I serve.

I serve to please, and to get the approval from an audience of one—God. In the end, I will stand before the Lord, not as a pastor's wife, but as myself, a sinner saved by His grace. Like the servant in the story of the talents, I want to stand before my Master and Lord and hear Him say, "Well done." Matthew 5:16 says, *"Let your light so shine before men, that they may see your good works, and glorify your Father which is in heaven."* I want this life that God has allowed me to live, to be used for His glory, for an eternal purpose, and I want to love Him with all my heart, and share that love with others.

Always be watchful with your conversation, how you speak to others about him or your communication with him. Occasionally, misunderstanding will arise concerning the congregation, leadership, financial matters, or just a simple misunderstanding or misjudgments; yet be careful with evil speaking. 1 Peter 2:1 says, "Let all bitterness and wrath and anger and clamor and slander be put away from you, along with all malice." Keep in mind he's your husband, pastor, lover, friend, confidant, and the father of your children—many roles in one person. So words can be sharp if not checked before spoken.

At times, a pastor needs to unload on someone he can trust. Besides Jesus, I do not know of anyone else who needs to be that person more than the wife of the pastor. Listen to him. Do not judge him. However, when he asks your opinion — and he will — always be honest with him. He may not always want to hear it, but in love, share honestly with him. Understand that when you approach him with an issue, your timing is also of utmost importance. Through the years, he will learn the value of your input. This does not mean that your perspective is always right any more than his, but together, process and pray. Grow together as you both walk through difficult times.

Every pastor has goals and ideals. A pastor should always be sure to attain an affirmative vote or approval from his wife. He should know he is never alone in success or failure. The pastor's wife is always under observation. Her support for her husband's ministry will be a positive contribution towards the building of the congregation's confidence in the leadership of her husband as the pastor.

Every man has visions and cherished dreams. Very often he may not be able to share this with anyone, not even his congregation, as the timing may not be right. However, if he has an understanding wife who has spiritual perception, he is able to share his visions and dreams with his wife, and then together, they can pray and work towards reaching their goals. To share his vision, is to grow with him in the ministry. It is the wife's responsibility to train herself to enlarge her vision, expanding herself concurrently with the growth of the church, and the growth of her husband's ministry. With growth comes changes and challenges, so be willing to accommodate those changes and challenges. Be flexible and willing to explore new avenues of ministry.

In many cases, the pastor's wife is the only church member who has been with him from the very beginning of his pastoral ministry, and will be with him until the end of his ministry. She has heard his first sermon, and possibly may be there when he preaches his last. Her opinions and positive criticisms are of great value, and any wise husband will take heed to his wife's constructive comments or criticisms.

—— Chapter 6 ——

GUARDING MY HEART AS HIS "BELOVEDMATE"

I AM MY BELOVED'S AND HIS DESIRE IS TOWARD ME *(SOS 7:10)*

My beloved is like a roe or a young hart: behold he standeth behind our wall, he looked forth at the windows, shewing himself through the lattice *(SOS 2:9)*

My beloved is mine and I am his; he browses among the lilies. *(SOS 2:16)*

My beloved spoke and said to me, arise my darling my beautiful one, come with me to me. *(SOS 2:10)*

And the Lord God caused a deep sleep to fall upon Adam and he slept and he took one of his ribs and closed up the rib which the Lord God had taken from man and he made a woman and bought her unto the man. Adam said this is now bone of my bones and flesh of my flesh; she shall be called woman because she was taken out of man. Therefore, shall a man leave his father and his mother and shall cleave unto his wife and they shall be one flesh *(Gen 2:21-25)*.

As a pastor's wife, you have to always be sensitive to the needs of your husband, bearing in mind that you are "twain," or one flesh. When one hurts, the other feels the pain. It is important that you know when he is hurting, and be watchful and prayerful as the Lord uses him.

When your husband has delivered his sermons, it is important that he has some quiet time with the Lord. During this time, you should cover him by praying over him, canceling any backlash, peradventure, or anything the enemy may be scheming. In your prayer, ask the Lord to close all doors, and to nullify the tricks and plans of the enemy.

After preaching, the enemy is always lurking for an open door, or an opportunity to come in and wreak havoc. In the same manner in which the serpent or the enemy beguiled Eve, the enemy will be seeking an opportunity to attack via the wife or via a third party.

A pastor and his wife should both be comfortable enough with one another to share their most intimate thoughts, and be able to express themselves without fear or intimidation. As pastors' wives, we need to understand that they are "male creatures," and have sexual needs and desires just like any other male.

Leading men such as pastors have so much on their minds, and are always giving of themselves; therefore, they need a wife who is a good communicator and listener. Your husband needs a wife who knows how to fulfill his sexual needs and desires, and for his wife to see it as a time of communion and fellowship, and not just "sex." If communication and fellowship is carried out, both parties will be satisfied, and the Lord will be glorified.

Some wives allow "third parties" to come into their marriage bed, by way of their husband watching pornographic movies. The reason for this may be, that the wife may not be sexually adventurous, or for whatever reason, her husband is not satisfied; but there is no legitimate excuse or reason to open such a door to the enemy. In 1 Corinthians 6:12, the Bible says, *"All things are lawful unto me, but all things are not expedient: all things are lawful for me, but I will not be brought under the power of any."*

There are pastors' wives who have had confrontations with women in the church, who they suspected, slept with their husband. Maybe it did not happen, but there are ways to deal with matters like this, without breaking up a church. Keep your sexual communication open with your husband, and learn his personal needs. Sadly, many wives in ministry are neglected. They long to have more time with their husband, but often feel guilty asking for it because by asking, they feel that they are insinuating that an important ministry priority should be neglected for her.

Do not feel tense or shy discussing sex with your husband. Many of the most conservative pastors' wives are more in tune on this subject than some of the most "liberated" females in the church. For some, young or old, conservative or liberated, sex is a heavy subject, and you need to lighten up!

If you have not learned to lighten up, your attitude probably makes you seem "motherly" or aged to your husband. What a turn off! You are not his mother, nor are you his spiritual authority. Lighten up! Quit being "Mother Superior." Start being the joyful playmate God intended you to be: "*Let her be as the loving hind and pleasant roe; let her breasts satisfy thee at all times; and be thou ravished always with her love*" (Proverbs 5:19).

Work on sex at home. *Drink waters out of thine own cistern and running waters out of thine own well* (Proverbs 5:15). If your husband is unresponsive, take your time, and keep at it with tenderness and compassion, until your sex life takes off. Plan a time to talk about sexual things. Try to find what excites his sexual interest. Do not hurry. Consider Christian counseling, and be patient. Do not forget your commitment to him, no matter what. Do not give up! The problem may not even be of a sexual nature. Work on all the other areas of your relationship. Focus your thoughts on him, not on other men. Give it time.

Remember to keep your own fire hot at home. Take care of yourself — at least, try. Take time to be romantic, especially throughout the day; go ahead and call him at his office and say something surprising!

Good sexual expression takes time and forethought. On special occasions, arrange for a hotel night as a getaway for fun, romance, rest and relaxation. Take time to listen to your husband. Learn to look him in the eyes. Flirt with your husband. Buy a surprising nighty to make yourself look attractive. Learn to relax! Learn to like and love yourself; develop confidence.

Learn what satisfies and excites your husband. Admire his physique, and compliment him on his physical attributes. Initiate things once in a while! Find out how he wants you to dress for him, and then do it!

Study your husband carefully to discover how you can light his fire. Study his likes and dislikes, his strengths and weaknesses, his moods and mannerisms. Just loving a man is fine but it's not enough. To live with one successfully, you have to know him, and to know him, you have to study him. You'll understand when your husband needs encouragement as well as when he needs to calm down and reflect more rationally.

Remember, you may not think of your husband as physically attractive anymore, but his position of power makes him a target for other women. Proverbs 7:26 says, *"For she hath cast down many wounded: yea, many strong men have been slain by her."*

"Nevertheless to avoid fornication, let every man have his own wife and let everywoman have her own husband. Let the husband render unto the wife due benevolence and likewise also the wife unto the husband, the wife hath not power over her own body but the husband and likewise also the husband hath not power of his own body but the wife. Defraud ye not one another except it be with consent for a time that ye may give your selves to fasting and prayer and come together that Satan tempt you not for your incontinency." (1Corinthians 7:3-5)

--------- *Chapter 7* ---------

PRAYING FOR
YOUR HUSBAND

"Pray always, with all prayer and supplication, in the Holy Spirit where you can quench all the fiery darts of the wicked" (Ephesians 6:18).

IT IS IMPORTANT THAT we stay in prayer before the Lord on our husband's behalf. You should be the principal intercessor, praying on your husband's behalf.

Practice submitting your spouse to the Lord daily. When he is on the pulpit ministering, it is essential for you to be his spiritual cheerleader, and for you to always be vigilant with spiritual eagle eyes, watching and praying. Praying always, does not mean you must always walk around praying with your physical eyes closed, but it means having your mind and thoughts in a spiritual position. Pray for your husband's heart to be filled with forgiveness, praise, thanksgiving, love, peace and joy because "*a good man, out of the good treasure of his heart, brings forth good things*" (Mathew 12:35).

1. Pray For Protection From Satan

Pray to keep your husband's mind sober. "*Be watchful. Your adversary the devil, prowls around like a roaring lion, seeking someone to devour*" (1 Peter 5:8).

If Satan can take down a shepherd of God's people, the odds are much higher that God's people will scatter, and they will become bitter and disenfranchised. They will question everything they have ever been taught by that pastor. Satan targets pastors because the damage is exponential if they fall. Pray for your husband that he would be kept safe from the schemes of Satan:

Father, please protect my husband from the attacks of Satan. Give him the strength to endure temptation and stand firm against the accusations Satan loves to whisper in his ear. Help him stand firm in your service, always fighting for the faith and for your people. I ask this is the name of Jesus. Amen.

2. Pray For His Protection Against His Own Heart

"If each person is tempted when he or she is lured and enticed by his own desire, then the desire, when it is conceived, gives birth to sin; sin, when it is fully grown, brings forth death" (James 1:14-15).

Pastors do not fall because one day, out of the blue, they just decide to dive headlong into sin. The descent into sin happens slowly over time, in small increments, as the pastor believes the lies presented to him by his flesh. Pray for your husband that he would be on guard against the prevarications of sin. Pray that he would have a saintly fear of God:

Father, please protect my husband from the deceitfulness of sin that we all are so prone to, and guard him from sin. Keep his conscience sensitive to the voice of your Holy Spirit. Keep him close to you, and close to your word, in the mighty name of Jesus. Amen.

3. Pray For Deep Spiritual Encouragement

"For I long to see you, that I may impart to you some spiritual gift to strengthen you— that is, that we may be mutually encouraged by each other's faith, both yours and mine" (Romans 1:11-12).

Pastoral ministry can be a brutal, discouraging work. Pastors find themselves in the midst of terrible situations on a regular basis: divorce, death, apostasy, and much more. It is also challenging because pastors do not see progress in the expedient manner in which other professions do. Christians are always progressing. As a result of this, discouragement and depression becomes a familiar companion to the minister if he is not covered in prayer. Pray for your husband to be encouraged:

*Father, please encourage my husband by the power
of your Holy Spirit. Let his soul be refreshed
with the love of Christ. Let him have faith for the
future. Help him to keep pressing forward, even
when the way is strewn with landmines. Lord,
let him be refreshed by the fact that your grace is
sufficient, in the name of Jesus. Amen.*

4. Pray For Wisdom

"If any of you lack wisdom, let him ask God, who
gives generously to all without reproach, and it will
be given him" (James 1:5).

Wisdom is the key in ministry that unlocks many
doors. Many elements of pastoral ministry are
not straightforward or clear-cut as black or white,
and so pastors require wisdom like Solomon's to
successfully maneuver through the murky gray
areas in life's circumstances. Your husband really
needs God's wisdom to deal with the issues of
the saints.

For example, a husband and wife are in seri-
ous conflict, and the husband would have one
story, while the wife would have a totally different

version of that story. Another example is, a church member needs financial support, but has a history of mismanaged finances. Additionally, a young man struggles with same-sex attraction, while still wanting to follow Jesus. Pastors need God's wisdom to navigate these gray areas sensitively, wisely and successfully. Pray that God give your husband a wealth of wisdom:

Father, please give my husband an outpouring of your wisdom which is perfect and holy. Help him know the way to go even when the way is not clear. Give him discernment to know good from evil, even when evil is dressed as good. Help him apply your word to even the most confusing situations, in the mighty name of Jesus Christ. Amen.

5. Pray For A Healthy Body

Paul said, "*I discipline my body and keep it under control, lest after preaching to others, I, myself, should be disqualified*" (1 Corinthians 9:27). Ministry can take a tremendous toll on a pastor's body. Yes, our bodies are temples, but they are more often than not, broken temples. Long nights at the hospital, high-stressed situations, and ever-present discouragement can quickly lead to burnout and bodily malfunction. Not only do pastors need spiritual strength, but they need physical strength as well. Pray for your husband— your pastor — that he would be sustained in his body and in his mind:

Father, please give my husband strength. Protect him from sickness and disease. Give him your supernatural energy to keep serving faithfully. Help him to find periods of rest and recovery. Guide him to still waters in the name of Jesus Christ. Amen.

6. Pray For A Strong Marriage And Family Unit

Therefore, an overseer must be above reproach, the husband of one wife, sober-minded, self-controlled, respectable, hospitable, and able to teach, not a drunkard, not violent but gentle, not quarrelsome, not a lover of money. He must manage his own household well, with all dignity, keeping his children submissive, for if someone does not know how to manage his own household, how will he care for God's church (1 Timothy 3:2-6).

Church history is littered with the skeletons of pastors whose marriages and families fell apart under the strain of pastoral ministry. As the above Bible text states, if a pastor can't manage his family, then how would he be able to manage the church of God? Satan loves to sabotage a pastor's family, and your pastor needs prayers that God will give him a healthy marriage and family life:

> *Father, please give us a healthy marriage. Strengthen the bonds between both of us as husband and wife. Encourage us both in ministry. Give both of us the wisdom to manage our family and to keep you at the center and not ministry. I also pray for our children that they will come to truly know you, follow you and be a beacon of light in the world, in the name of Jesus Christ. Amen!*

7. Pray For Meaningful Friendships

"A man of many companions may come to ruin, but there is a friend who sticks closer than a brother" (Proverbs 18:24).

Pastoral ministry can be surprisingly lonely. There is something about being in a position of leadership that isolates the man. People look to him to be a teacher and leader, but not be their close friend. Pastors need close friends who will encourage them, hold them accountable, and push them toward Christ. Pray that your husband will have friends as such:

> *Father, please give my husband true, deep, sustaining friendships. Not fleshy relationships, but spiritual bonds as laborers together with God. Give him friends who stick closer than brothers, in Jesus' name. Amen!*

Let us identify some other important areas of maturity that are necessary in every pastor's wife. We might begin with prayerfulness and reachability. Every pastor's wife will be privy to information and the burdens of the ministry beyond the scope of the average church member. That information, particularly during times of trial, will be either a source of sanctification or a source of cynicism and bitterness against the church.

Therefore, a pastor's wife must develop a robust life of prayer. As a "helper suitable" to the work of her husband, she needs to realize that this is one of the key areas of co-laboring with him in the work that the Lord has called him to do. Along with prayerfulness, she needs to have a teachable spirit—always. Through the tests and triumphs of ministry, not only will you need to be constantly growing as a pastor's wife, but you will also need to keep your husband in prayer before the Lord.

--- *Chapter 8* ---

PASTORS' WIVES AND THEIR LIFESTYLE

"Who can find a virtuous woman, for her price is far above rubies" (Proverbs 31).

I DO NOT BELIEVE THE "First Lady" lifestyle should be a worldly showpiece, or that a pastor's wife should carry a proud look; rather, she should be graceful, walking in her own uniqueness, style and purpose. You may not have the beauty of Queen Esther, but God has made all creatures beautiful—we are all fearfully and wonderfully made!

Many church folks and pastors' wives think the lifestyle of a pastor's wife should be portrayed as that of a celebrity: driving the latest car, dressing up every Sunday in a new outfit, with a matching hat, shoe, handbag and a lace handkerchief, and a new hairdo, along with nails properly manicured. This may look impressive, but this is only the outward appearance. Also, many pastor's wives cannot attain this life style because of their financial income, or lack thereof. Every wife is on a different level, and they grow to different measures or levels as the Lord blesses them.

I just want to encourage you leading ladies to be who you are, and to walk in your position and purpose with grace and humility. It is okay not to have your own car, or to not have parking spot labeled "Reserved" for you at church. Just wait on your season of blessings. It is fine if you drive a Mitsubishi.

Meeting or exceeding the dress code, and having an abundance of material things do not determine the level of your spiritual growth, your effectiveness, your success in ministry, or who you are as a pastor's wife, mother and woman. Be content and faithful with what the Lord has blessed you with; be at the level God has you until He grants you increase in prosperity. You shall reap if you faint not!

The only place in the scripture that describes a dress code to the women in the church is found in Titus Chapter 2: "*Let it be the hidden man which is of a great price.*" The scripture tells us to put more emphasis on the hidden man, which is our spirit man, than we do our physical appearance and material possessions.

In outlining the basic principles of how one should dress, it is established that one should not feel convicted about any part of an outfit; whether it is because the outfit is a source of pride, because it is too revealing, or for some other reason. None of these can be codified as an absolute or official standard; different people will feel convicted about different things.

Whatever these "convictions" are, they are to be avoided as much as possible. This situation is similar to that in the Bible, in which persons were asserting that they should not eat meat, and Paul gave them instructions in 1 Corinthians 8:10

and in Romans 14:10 — *"But why dost thou judge thy brother or why dost thou set at nought thy brother? For we shall all stand before the judgment seat of Christ."*

There are many hurting preachers' wives who are dressing to impress others. Whether we realize it or not, the pastor's wife sets the tone or the standard for all the other ladies in the congregation with her style or manner of dress. Whether the women in the congregation admit it or not, they are watching you.

I have seen many pastors' wives wear the big hats, but in actuality some of them are wearing a mask to cover up the fact that they are wounded and lonely. This can be a challenge for many wives because their husbands are spending too much time at the church, and not enough time with her and the family. This can bring about bitterness and hatred towards the congregation.

It takes a "special lady" and "a GRACE "to undertake and manage such an awesome task of being a pastor's wife. Many others think it is fame or fortune to be a pastor's wife. More often than not, being a pastor's wife is not a frontline ministry, but rather, a ministry in which you pray and work behind the scenes.

Many ladies see being a pastor's wife as a "glamorous seat," whereby you sit in a large, beautiful chair, looking pretty and smiling, and looking like "church royalty" from the pew while you are being served. You need to know how to pray in the Holy Spirit and do warfare. Also, you must remember, the highest position in God's Kingdom is that of a servant.

Your virtuous character and respect is very paramount; your husband wants and needs this from you. Spend more time enhancing your intellect, and developing and strengthening your spirit man than you do in adorning your outward man.

If we are given the privilege and the opportunity to be a pastor's wife, let our lifestyle and behavior reflect our spiritual walk. We are representatives of the bride of Christ, and we, as the wife of the pastor, represent a "special bride" who the ministry looks up to. We should not confuse people with our behavior and lifestyle through contradicting who and what God has called us to be.

Pastor's wives should never compare themselves with anyone. They should accept who they are and whose they are. "*For we are not bold to class or compare ourselves with some of those who commend themselves, but when they measure themselves by themselves and compare themselves with themselves they are without understanding"* (2 Corinthians 10:12). If we are always comparing ourselves with other ladies, we will never be content and thankful. There will always be someone you see as being more beautiful than you are, more attractively or fashionably dressed than you do, or someone who has more material things than you do.

However, we must accept ourselves for who we are, accept where we are, and accept what we have and currently do not have. All of us have strength and weaknesses. Let us not beat ourselves down because someone has a gift we do not have. We should complement one another, and we must celebrate one another.

Stop comparing your possessions, appearance, performance and circumstances to other persons', and start living the way God intended for you to live. Be thankful for being different! Psalms 139:14 says, *"I will praise thee, for I am fearfully and wonderfully made. Marvelous are thy works and that my soul knows very well."* The next time you find yourself making comparisons, remind yourself that you are fearfully and wonderfully made. Let that sink in: you are one of a kind—a masterpiece!

Seek approval from God, not man. 2 Timothy 2:15 says, "*Do your best to present yourself to God as one approved, a worker who has no need to be ashamed, rightly handling the word of truth.*" Remind yourself often of all that you are in Christ Jesus, and discover the freedom that comes without comparisons.

Examples of Pastors' Wives Lifestyle
Scenario 1

Many pastors' wives have mixed feelings about having a housekeeper and a baby sitter to assist them with household chores. They often think they are able to clean and maintain their homes themselves especially if it's a large home. If you can afford a maid, it can help especially if you are a pastor's wife with few small children and has a full time job. Getting someone in the home few times a week can help you organized your schedules.

Scenario 2

She is a veteran teacher who started her teaching career as a spinster, and during the course of her life, she has acquired various teaching skills.

One thing many can attest to, is the fact that she loves being modest in all facets; she does not like being flamboyant like her husband. She tailored a style for herself that is perfect to her fit and liking. Any time she is spotted, one is bound to see her dressed often in a skirt suit, and a hat to match. She makes sure that whatever she wears, depicts her as a woman of desirable quality, not only externally, but more so, inwardly. The hat has become her "trademark." Although, she is chauffeured everywhere, she prefers automobiles that are not gaudy because of her Bible-based beliefs. It is also rare to see her wearing jewellery or make-up.

Scenario 3

This pastor's wife can pass for a beauty queen. She is easy-going and quite natural. She is blessed with three children. She is a stylish woman of excellence. She drives a Range Rover that has a personalized registration number. She is blessed with a good figure, and has wonderful skin. Also, she knows how to put her outfits together. She loves modest jewellery.

Just as God wants His Church to be glorious, without spot or wrinkle, and without blemish, so, too, a woman should maintain or properly manage her physical appearance. She should do so, not only for herself and for her husband, but also out of respect for the symbolism God is using her to represent in the Kingdom.

So, when you, as a woman dress, you should accentuate your beauty, knowing that your physical beauty is symbolic of the spiritual beauty of Christ's bride, the Church. You dress first, and foremost, to please God and to show the beauty of His creation, which is *you*!

~

I hope, as a Pastor's wife, you will search the Scriptures, and then discuss your findings respectfully with your husband. If you need to make changes, then make them. Know that God wants the best in all areas of your life. Dressing beautifully and appropriately for the occasion is what God has called you to do. Do not hide the beautiful work of art that God has made, but display it in ways that please both God and your husband.

In summarizing it all, dressing modestly, biblically speaking, does not specifically mean "dressing in an unappealing or unattractive way." It means to dress appropriately for the occasion. So, while it may be perfectly acceptable for you to wear a bikini to the beach, it would not be appropriate for you to wear a bikini to a job interview or to a church service.

As pastors' wives, we want to be watchful over our finances; how we spend money and our love for money. Paul warns us that the love of money is the root of all kinds of evil (1 Timothy 6:10). He urges Timothy to be content with a little more than food and clothing, and warns him that those who desire to be rich, fall into temptation (1 Timothy 6:8–9). Paul then instructs Timothy to flee from such love of money (1 Timothy 6:11). A pastor who has been called by God will be compelled to serve the church, whether it leads to personal gain or not. However, if his wife does not share in that same love and burden-bearing for the church, the financial sacrifices that often go along with ministry, may become a source of bitterness for her.

A pastor's wife must focus on developing an attitude of contentment. Sometimes she will have to watch other people in the church, do things with their children that she is not able to do with her children. She will have to watch them decorate their homes in ways she cannot afford to decorate her home. She will have to see others purchasing things that she and her family cannot afford, but she must understand that the rewards of ministry do not always come in the form of tangible things or in monetary form. To be clear, Paul urges churches to generously support their pastors (1 Timothy 5:17), but many churches will struggle to do that out of a lack of resources, or a lack of spiritual maturity. Unless, or until church members grow in both of these areas, a pastor's wife must guard herself against a materialistic outlook that fails to see the riches of a joyful marriage, and the privilege of serving others. Do not place too much value on the riches of this world.

Chapter 9

SERVING,
DISCIPLINE AND
COMMUNICATION

EVERYONE IS GIFTED BY God for a special work in His kingdom. Do not assume the pastor's wife will have the same gifts as "all other pastors' wives." I can almost guarantee that she will not. Remember that the term "pastor's wife" does not occur anywhere in scripture. God does not have a list of qualifications for her, like He does for bishops, deacons or pastors. Thus, she needs freedom and time with the Lord to find her niche in the ministry.

One of the most important and overlooked persons in a church is the pastor's wife. She is usually not included in the organizational chart. She does not have a formal job description, and she is an unpaid volunteer. However, her ministry can make or break her family and church. The pastor's wife is the last to sit down when there is a church-family meal because she wants to ensure that everyone is served. Many times she is busy looking after everyone else.

Often, she is the last person to get her husband's undivided attention because his phone is always ringing with someone on the other end, who has knowingly or unknowingly decided they are more important than her. Pastors' wives have to be confident about who they are, and open to loving all people.

You are obligated to be loyal to the congregation. Disloyalty shows up in gossip. Do not listen to things of the past, nor allow someone from the congregation (or from anywhere) to gossip about your husband, or about anyone in your presence.

Experience is the only teacher that gives you the test first, without you having studied. There is great wisdom in the love of discipline, which I must confess, goes against the grain of our culture and our human nature. However, the refusal of discipline or reproof leads to stupid decisions that can cause us a lot of pain and grief. I would rather be corrected than to be incorrect any day.

There is so much in the Bible about discipline. I did find that the common thread in discipline is God's love. You cannot separate love from discipline because discipline is evidence of love. You never discipline those you do not love, but the ones you never discipline are like the ones you do not love, or at least, love enough.

Servanthood requires a mental shift, a change in your attitude. God is always more interested in *why* we do something, than He is in *what* we do. Attitude counts more than achievements. King Amaziah lost God's favor because he did what was right in the sight of the Lord, yet not with a true heart.

Do not compare, criticize, or compete with other pastors' wives. They are too busy doing the work God has given them. Competition between

God's servants is illogical for many reasons: we're all on the same team; our goal is to make God look good, not ourselves; we have been given different assignments; and we're all uniquely created. Paul said we should not compare ourselves with one another, as if one of us is better, and the other is worse. We have far more interesting things to do with our lives. Each of us is an original—a masterpiece!

There is no place for petty jealousy between servants. When you are busy serving, you do not have time to be critical or jealous. Any time spent criticizing others, is time that could have been spent ministering to others. When Martha complained to Jesus that Mary was not helping with the work, this revealed that she had lost her servant's heart. Real servants do not complain about unfairness; they do not have pity-parties, nor do they resent those not serving. They trust God and keep serving.

It is not our job to evaluate other servants. The Bible says, "Who are you to criticize someone else's servant?" The Lord will determine whether His servant has been successful. It is also not our job to defend ourselves against criticism. Let your

Master handle it. Follow the example of Moses who showed true humility in the face of opposition, as did Nehemiah, whose response to critics was simply, "My work is too important to stop now and visit with you."

If you serve like Jesus, you can expect to be criticized. The world, and even much of the church, does not understand what God values. The disciples criticized one of the most beautiful acts of love shown to Jesus: Mary took the most valuable thing she owned, expensive perfume, and poured it over Jesus. Her lavish service was called "a waste" by the disciples, but Jesus called it "significant," and that is all that matters. Your service or sacrifice for Christ is never wasted, regardless of what others say.

If you are going to be a servant, you must settle your identity in Christ. Only secure people can serve. The more insecure you are, the more you will want people to serve you, and the more you will need their approval. On the other hand, when you base your worth and identity on your relationship with Christ, you are freed from the expectations of others. You are free to serve without borders!

Just enjoy helping people, meeting needs, and doing ministry. "Serve the Lord with gladness." Why do we serve with gladness? We serve with gladness because we love the Lord; we are grateful for His grace; we know serving is the highest use of life, and God has promised a reward. Jesus promised that the Father will honor and reward anyone who serves Him. Paul added, He will not forget how hard you have worked for Him, and how you have shown your love for Him by caring for other Christians.

A pastor's wife need to have genuine love for the church, which means a genuine love for the people entrusted to the care of her husband and the elders of the church. It is the kind of love that will not resent when she sends her husband off in the middle of the night, or when her husband must take extra time in the evenings to counsel a couple. Her love for God's sheep gives her joy because she loves the people God has given to the care of her husband. She does not resent their need for his attention when needed. Equally as important, she can be the key to communicating this kind of joy to her children, so that they view these things, not as a burden, but as an opportunity to participate in the ministry of the church by sacrificing family time to serve the needs of people.

"He who finds a wife, finds a good thing" (Proverbs 18:22). A church that finds a pastor with a well-prepared wife, finds a hidden treasure they were probably not even seeking. Too often, it is not so much the pastor, but rather his wife, who indirectly makes or breaks his ministry. Ask any fruitful pastor about the keys to the strength of his ministry, and he will inevitably say that the Lord has granted him abundant grace, by giving him a wife who has faithfully loved him and the church because she has supremely loved the Lord above all else.

Chapter 10

MAINTAINING BALANCE WITHIN THE DEMANDS OF MINISTRY AND FAMILY

Busyness, or an out-of-balance life, is a constant threat to our intimacy with God, our marriage, our family and other important relationships. If we are not careful, the urgent needs of the church will overtake our lives. I have found this to be a challenge for most pastors' wives, but it is possible to maintain a balance;

and balance is necessary for the spiritual and emotional health of the pastor and his family.

Most pastors and their wives have children. Sundays are typically very busy days in a pastor's home. Your Sundays begin from Saturday night: preparing meals and clothing, ensuring everyone is looking great, and that they will be able to eat a home-cooked meal right after church. Most Sunday mornings, the pastor's wife has so many "caps to wear," or roles to play. Some families begin with early prayer at the church, some have Sunday school, and then morning worship, and other families have to attend evening services.

Many pastors and their wives drive or fly into different city locations to attend two to three services every week. The congregation expects to see the pastor's wife attend all of these services. So, in most instances, the wife has to prepare breakfast if the husband desires to eat, and she has to feed the family or younger children who cannot take care of themselves. In many cases, the wife must prepare dinner in between all of the aforementioned activities.

She must ensure she has prayed for everyone, including her husband, who will be presenting the word of God. When all these "chores" are completed, everyone is expecting her to get dressed, and to be on time, looking perfect in appearance with a big smile on her face, ready to serve all.

The list of assignments a pastor's wife does before she comes to church, and after she arrives, is enough "to call her duty done" for that day.

A pastor's wife is simply a Christian church member like everyone else. Her first priorities are to be a godly Christian woman, wife and mother. Then, all other duties can follow.

A pastor's wife does not have to be directly involved in church assignments that will keep her away from her home and her family. When your children are young, it is important that you schedule yourself to spend quality time with them because they ask for their parents when they do not see much of them. We cannot get too busy in church, and forget that we have a husband and children who need us. In many instances, some things are church ministry, and not Kingdom ministry—there is a difference. Do not let church ministry burn you out, and then when it is time for Kingdom ministry, you are too tired.

Tension, confusion, frustration, and even spiritual defeat can confront a pastor's wife when she is trying to balance church ministry and home ministry. Home ministry is the God-given role we have as wives who love our spouses as God loves us. If we are parents, it includes our role to love and raise our children according to God's truth. The Bible commands us to invest in our spouse and children by nurturing them, helping them develop intellectually, physically, relationally, and spiritually. I will tell you of a prophecy:

I will utter dark sayings of old, which we have heard and known, and our fathers have told us. We will not hide them from their children; we will show to the generation to come, the praises of the Lord, and his strength, and his wonderful works that he hath done. For God established a testimony in Jacob and appointed a law in Israel, which he commanded our fathers to make known to their children. That the generation to come might know them, even the children which should be born, who should arise and declare them to their children. That they might set their hope in God, and not forget the works of God, but keep his commandments (Psalms 78:2-7).

This requires maintaining an intimate relationship with each family member through consistent time with one another. Sometimes we experience a frequent sense of guilt when we go out to minister or fellowship. If we are leaving our spouse at home to do ministry, it somehow seems wrong, or we fear we are shortchanging our children when we leave them with a baby-sitter. It becomes even worse if our spouse or children beg us not to go out; they try to convince us to "please stay at home."

Remember these tensions are common, but can develop into a problem if we choose the family as our highest value in life! The family is not the highest value in life (a surprise to many), our relationship with God is. True, there is probably no greater blessing and joy than quality time spent with your Christ-centered family, but it is not an end unto itself. The family stands to serve God (Matthew 6:33). God wants us and our children to be committed to Him foremost, and then through His love, guidance, and power, we can love the family (Mark 12:29). "*If any man comes to me, and hates his father and mother, and wife and children, and brethren and sisters, yea and his own life also, he cannot be my disciple.*" (Luke 14:26).

The mature woman of God, will trust God to meet her needs while serving others. I want my children to know that they are terribly important to me, and that I love them and their father deeply. However, I do not want them to believe that they are the center of the universe, and that I, or anyone else, should live to love and serve *only* them. We must all teach and demonstrate to our children that God will care for us as we remain focused on serving and meeting the needs of others, then we will see God working powerfully in our families.

We quickly learn that ministry is far from a Monday-to-Friday job. When ministry is done with passion, it can be very demanding on one's schedule. That is not to say that we cannot find a proper balance of personal, family and work schedules, but that schedules often look very different from almost everyone's schedule in the church. The weekend, which for most families is a time of relaxation and socialization, is often the busiest and weightiest time of the week for a pastor's wife. There can be a wedding and a funeral on the same day of a given weekend. Even if you do not attend these events with your husband, he is still missing from around the home and from the family. This does not include the unforeseen events such as urgent prayers, or hospital visits. A wife must understand this, and she must be willing to forgo some of the activities that many other families might participate in during weekends.

Normally, as a pastor's wife, you grow in your experience and maturity, and you will have more capacity or time to do things on the weekend. A pastor's wife must understand this is a necessary process in the growth, and ministry of her husband. She must understand that the preaching event is the most important, single event in the life of the church each week. That means that the time in prayer and preparation leading up to that event, must take priority over many other things. With good communication (often early communication), your husband can arrange his schedule with you in advance. A pastor's wife needs to embrace the responsibility and weightiness of her husband's ministry.

How To Point Out Mistakes To Your Husband If You Must.

There are times when mistakes should be pointed out, and you may be the only person who cares enough to do this. When this is done properly, your husband should not resent it. Learn just how far you can go with him, where sensitive areas are, and where the difference lies between inciting anger and talking things out. When some wives criticize their husbands even in the slightest way, it signals an all-out war. Others can gently point out something they believe will help and it will be taken kindly. Guard your manner and tone of voice. Do not speak to your spouse as a parent punishing a small child for naughty behavior.

Your relationship with one another is more important than any relationship you hold with anyone else on earth including your children, so guard it carefully. Husband and wife should always feel free to discuss whatever disturbs them but it shouldn't be in the form of a direct attack. The surest way to weaken affection is to tell someone what is wrong with him too often. Nothing destroys love more quickly than a running account of faults. In order to feel loved, we must feel understood, not criticized or condemned.

RESOURCE MATERIALS

Conversations Over Coffee: First Ladies

CONVERSATION OVER COFFEE: FIRST Ladies Self-care Ministry!

- Our Yearly Dental–Medical Appointments

- Personal Get Always

- First Ladies Retreats

- Exercise/Spa treatments

- Beauty/Nail shop

- Mall Shopping

- Quiet Time Alone

- Ladies Night-out

TEN UNJUST HIGH EXPECTATIONS FOR THE PASTOR'S WIFE

THE WIVES OF PASTORS in many churches carry heavy burdens. Sometimes these heavy burdens are in the form of impossible expectations. So, what are some of these unfair expectations? The following are some comments I have received from pastors' wives over the years. Here are the top ten unrealistic expectations imposed upon these ladies:

1. I am expected to attend every function at church. – Always be yourself and do not feel the pressure to impress your congregation.

2. Many church members expect me to know everything that is happening in the church. – Pastors' wives are not expected to know everything their pastor/husband knows. For instance, some administrative matters are meant for the pastor and the elders.

3. We have several church members who feel free to complain to me about my husband. – Deal with emotional intelligence.

4. Church members utilize me as a mediator to my husband, giving me messages for him, after-services.

5. I am still amazed how many church members expect me to function as an employee of the church; doing everything and being busy.

6. Some of the members expect our children to be perfect and act perfect. Pastor's children (PK) have much pressure fitting into the congregation.

7. I am always supposed to be perfectly made up and dressed up when I leave the house. Church members voice their disappointment and disapproval to a pastor's wife who ran into a grocery store without makeup.

8. I have no freedom at our church to be anything, but perfect and emotionally composed. – Many pastors' wives live in pretense and try to be tough cookies. Feel

free to cry or express your emotions at a given season.

9. Some church members expect my family to live in poverty all our lives (referring to the criticism received for purchasing items not meeting their expectation or need upgrade quicker).

10. So many church members expect me to be their best friend. – You cannot be everyone's best friend.

Words Of Wisdom To Pastors/Ministers' Wives

1. Never raise your voice for any reason to your husband. It's a sign of disrespect. Prov 15:1 – *A GENTLE answer turns away wrath but a harsh word stirs up anger.*

2. Don't expose your husband's weaknesses to your family and friends. It will bounce back at you. You are each other's keeper. Eph 5:12 – *For it is shameful even to mention what the disobedient do in secret.*

3. Never use attitudes and moods to communicate to your husband, you never know how your husband will interpret them. Defensive women don't have a happy home. Prov 15:13 – *A joyful heart makes a cheerful face, but when the heart is sad the spirit is broken.*

4. Never compare your husband to other men; you have no idea what their life is all about.

If you attack his ego, his love for you will diminish.

5. Never ill-treat your husband's friends because you don't like them. The person who's supposed to get rid of them is your husband. Prov 11:22 – *Like a gold ring in a pigs snout is a beautiful woman who shows no discretion.*

6. Never forget that your husband married you, not your maid or anyone else. Do your duties. Gen 2:24 – *For this reason a man will leave his father and mother and be united to his wife and they will become one flesh.*

7. Never assign anyone to give attention to your husband, people may do everything else but your husband is your own responsibility. Eph 5:33 – *Nevertheless let each individual among you also love his own wife even as himself and let the wife see to it that she respects her husband.*

8. Never blame your husband if he comes back home empty-handed. Rather encourage him. Deut 3:28 – *But charge Joshua and encourage and strengthen him for he shall go over before this people*

and he shall cause them to possess the land which
you shall see.

9. Never be a wasteful wife, your husband's sweat is too precious to be wasted.

10. Never pretend to be sick for the purpose of denying your husband sex. You must give it to him how he wants it. Sex is very important to men. No man can withstand sex starvation for too long (even the anointed ones). SOS 7:12 – *Let us get up early to the vineyards let us see if the vine flourish, whether the tender grape appear and the pomegranates bud forth there will I give thee my loves.*

11. Never compare your husband to your one-time sex mate in bedroom, or an ex-lover. SOS 5:9 – *What is thy beloved more than another beloved, O thou fairest among women? What is thy beloved more than another beloved that thou dost so charge us?*

12. Never answer for your husband in public opinion polls, let him handle what is directed to him although he may answer for you in public opinion polls. Prov. 31:23 – *Her*

husband is known in the city gates when he sits among the elders of the land.

13. Never shout or challenge your husband in front of children. Wise women don't do that. Eph 4:31 – *Let all bitterness and indignation and wrath (passion, rage, bad temper) and resentment (anger, animosity) and quarreling (brawling, clamor contention) and slander (evil speaking abusive or blasphemous language be banished from you, with all malice (spite ill will or baseness of any kind).*

14. Be a virtuous woman who is a crown to her husband. Prov 12:4 – *A wife of noble character is her husband's crown but a disgraceful wife is like decay in his bones.*

15. Be watchful with inviting friends who want to hang around your home all the time.

16. Never be in a hurry adorning yourself for your husband. Most women take time out to look attractive. 1 Sam 25:3 – *Now the man's name was Nabal and his wife name was Abigail. And the woman was intelligent and beautiful in appearance but the man was harsh and evil in his dealings and he was a calebite.*

17. Your parents or family or friends do not have the final say in your marriage. Don't waste your time looking up to them for a final word. You must leave if you want to cleave. Luke 21:16 – *You will be betrayed even by parents, brother's relatives and friends and they will put some of you to death.*

18. Never base your love on monetary things.

19. Don't forget that husbands want attention and are good listeners. Good communication is the bedrock of every happy home. Gal 6:9 – *Let us not become weary in doing well, for at the proper time we will reap a harvest if we do not give up.*

20. If your idea worked better than his, never compare yourself to him. It's always teamwork. Gal 6:10 – *So then while we have opportunity let us do well to all men and especially to those who are of the household of the faith.*

21. Don't be too judgmental toward your husband. No man wants a nagging wife. Eph 4:29 – *Let no corrupt communication proceed out*

of your mouth but that which is good to the use of edifying that it may minister grace unto the hearers.

22. A lazy wife is a careless wife. She doesn't even know that her body needs a bath. Prov. 24:27 – *Prepare thy work without and make it fit for thyself in the field and afterward build thine house.* Prov. 20:13 – *Love not sleep, lest you come to poverty, open your eyes and you will be satisfied with bread.*

23. Does your husband like a kind of cooked food? Try to change your cooking to surprise him. Prov. 31:14 – *She is like the merchant ships, bringing her food from afar.*

24. Never be too demanding to your husband, enjoy every moment, resource as it comes. Luke 11:3 – *Give us each day our daily bread.*

25. Fruit of the womb is a blessing from the Lord, love your children and teach them well. Prov. 22:6 – *Train a child in the way he should go and when he is old he will not turn from it.*

26. You are never too old to influence your home.

27. A prayerful wife is a better equipped wife, prayer always for your husband and family. 1 Thess. 5:17 – *Pray without ceasing.*

Frequently Asked Questions and Answers for Pastors' Wives

QUESTION: Do all pastors' wives automatically become the co-Pastor of the church?

ANSWER: All pastors' wives are not called to co-pastor; however, there are some who are called in the office of co-pastor. Few of them are appointed by their husband at the beginning of the ministry, and some pastors' wives later find out that it is not the Lord's calling for them to occupy such an office. Also, interestingly, many women are actually the pastor of the church, and the husband is the co-pastor. A pastor's wife should always be at his side to assist with serving God's people.

QUESTION: Does a pastor's wife have to be out to each and every church service?

ANSWER: She is not obligated to attend *every* service, but it is good accountability and manners for her husband to apologize on her behalf when she is absent for a long period of time.

QUESTION: Should the pastor's wife sit on the pulpit with her husband, or is she obligated to sit in the front row, or in a special chair?

ANSWER: The pastor's wife should be able to sit wherever she is most comfortable, or she can sit in an assigned seat; it's "home" for her.

QUESTION: Is the pastor's wife obligated to be the church women's president?

ANSWER: No, she is not obligated to be the president, but she can oversee the work by having a great relationship with the women's president.

QUESTION: Is it biblical to call the wife of a pastor, elder, or bishop the "first lady" of the church?

ANSWER: The practice of calling the wife of the pastor of a local church "First Lady" of the church, does not come from the Bible. No precedent for it can be found in God's word, and the practice is in fact antithetical to such principles as servanthood and impartiality among followers of Christ.

Twenty Things Pastors' Wives Want You to Know About Them

1. She is not perfect at anything.

2. She is a normal woman like you. She has emotions, hobbies, and dreams. She enjoys pursuing interests outside of church just like you do.

3. She does not have to attend every event, or be on every committee to be a good pastor's wife. Family comes first, and sometimes priorities have to be rearranged.

4. When she has to confront an issue, it does not mean that she dislikes someone, or that she thinks she is better than them. Rather, it means she has spent time in prayer, and sought godly counsel on how to wisely handle the issue.

5. While she is expected to have tough skin (and she does), criticism still hurts deeply. The decisions she makes (with her husband) are not thoughtless, selfish ones. They are decisions made through prayer and made for the good of the church, and with the future in mind.

6. She desires to have friends. However, a pastor's wife has to maintain boundaries in order to minister to many ladies. She just doesn't want to hurt other women by doing so. Some of her best friends are other pastors' wives. Let her nurture those relationships that help keep her strengthened and refreshed.

7. When the phone rings at home, she always wonders (on the way to answer it) how that call will change her day, or even her life. She feels guilty to ever take the phone off the hook.

8. She often changes plans and gives up personal time with her husband because one of the flocks needs the pastor. She has

adjusted to having a husband who is an "on call pastor," much like a doctor.

9. She has children just like yours. They are not perfect. They are typical children.

10. She desires to have spiritual fellowship with other ladies.

11. When a church member passes away, she grieves as if it were a family member. Assisting at the funeral of a church member is one of the hardest things she will ever do.

12. She has trials and struggles that are not church related. She often bears those burdens alone, sometimes setting them aside to bear the burdens of other ladies.

13. When you take the time to encourage her and to be interested in her life, it means the world to her. She treasures the special notes, phone calls and tokens of appreciation.

14. When you come to her with a problem that needs counseling, she aches with you. She feels honored to pray with you, and to help you. She prays often for your success.

15. She does not have a flawless walk with God. She strives to have a close relationship with God, but she sins and falls short just like you do.

16. Sunday is not a day off. It is a very busy day for the pastor's family.

17. She strives to fulfill the expectations of God for her life.

18. She loves ministering to women; it is a passion. She would be disappointed if she was unable to minister to women—this is the heart God has given her.

19. She is the pastor's wife—not you.

20. She loves you more than you know.

Seven Things Pastors' Wives Wished They Had Been Told Before They Became the Wife of a Pastor

1. I wish someone had told me to just be myself.

2. I wish someone had prepared me to deal with criticism directed towards my husband and me.

3. I wish someone had reminded me that my husband is still, only human.

4. I wish someone had told me that others are *always* watching us.

5. I wish someone had told me there are some really mean people in the church.

6. I wish someone had told me exactly how much my husband needs me to build him up.

7. I wish someone had told me that my daily schedule will *never* be normal again.

Personal Issues Pastors' Wives Face and Words of Wisdom

1. Experiencing Superficial Relationships in the Church

Find relationships outside of the church. It is healthy to have your own friends who see you for who you are, and not solely as the wife of a pastor.

Join a pastors' wives group where you can share, laugh and talk about real issues with women who can relate. You can also join a book club, volunteer in civic or community groups, or do volunteer work in marketplace ministries.

2. Having a Busy Husband

Your husband will be busy! Do not be ashamed to ask him to set aside time for you, and you alone. Make it a priority for both of you, and do not budge on it unless there is an emergency. It is difficult to put the ministry work aside, but your marriage relationship will benefit.

3. Encountering Unkind Church Members

Some people can be mean, and they expect you and your family to be perfect, even though they certainly are not. They will hold you and your family to a higher standard than they do their own family and themselves. They will leave you out of their social circles, try to provoke you, gossip about you and the list goes on.

Sometimes, just being kind to these people, takes the steam out of their hatefulness. Realize what expectations are realistic and which ones are not. Be kind, and realize that sometimes, people are just going to be mean.

4. Being a Conduit for Complaints about Your Husband

When a person comes to you with complaints regarding your husband, redirect them by asking them to talk with one of the elders about the matter.

5. Date Nights

Make a commitment with your husband for a date night once a week – no matter what! Date nights spice up the marriage, and keep the marriage fresh and interesting. Date nights also give you and your husband something to look forward to within the week. Even if you have a date night in, make it special, and time focused only on just you and him – a time without any distractions.

6. Complaints about Your Children

This is such a difficult thing to deal with because people will expect your children to be perfect. Having two sons, while being a pastor's wife was a joy to me, but it came with times of testing. Sometimes people expect your children to be in church every time the doors open (just to please the congregation). However, there are times when they do not desire to go out on a given Sunday or Wednesday night, and some persons think our children "have sinned and come short of God's glory" because they missed a church service.

The saints expect our children to be well behaved all the time, always dressed immaculately in coat and necktie, just like the pastor. Remember, these are young people, and their style of dress is starkly different from ours as adults; therefore, do not judge them, let them be themselves and allow God to do His work inside of them and through them.

7. Your Husband Does Not Give You Priority

In whatever profession a man is in, he will be devoted to that profession because he has a God-given drive to work and to provide for his family. Sometimes this comes at the expense of the ones he truly loves.

Helping a church leader understand that his responsibilities at home are equally as important as his ministerial work, can be difficult, and often this comes up only after there is a crisis. Talk openly with your husband about your needs, and don't stop talking about it until he understands. Encourage him to seek accountability from other spiritual leaders or advisors in effort to restore balance to how he divides his time among his various responsibilities.

There are no easy answers, other than loving him strongly and caring deeply for him. Be sensitive to the challenges he experiences being in the ministry.

8. Experiencing Financial Struggles

Financial issues are tough because there is no easy way to talk about them. Often, churches do not provide well enough for their pastors financially.

This may put the pastor and his family in a position where the wife must work, and/or the pastor has to take on a second job. This especially rings true in a small church, where the tithes and offerings given may not be sufficient to cover expenses. The pastor should keep the elders or board members aware of the church's finances, so they have the full scope of the church's financial situation.

These issues have affected many women whose husbands are in ministry. Pray about them. Give them to God, and try to implement some of these suggestions; it will make a difference in your life, marriage and ministry.

COMMON CHALLENGES PASTORS' WIVES FACE

As with any job, there are challenges and struggles that come with being a pastor's wife. The difference is, the challenges that I face are as a direct result of my husband's occupation, not mine. In my opinion, this is often the reason why pastors' wives struggle with their role. The lack of control over their lives, which, if not handled well, can lead to resentment, bitterness, and rebellion against God.

Having spoken to many pastors' wives over the years, I have found that we all share a common experience, and therefore, common struggles. These are challenges that we are trying to work through in "a God-honoring way," but they are challenges nonetheless. The following are some of these challenges:

Loneliness and Isolation: Most people may look at you strangely when you say this, but it is probably the most common challenge for pastors' wives. It does not matter if they are in a small country church, or a megachurch in a major city. I have thought about the reasons for this many times because I have experienced it myself.

The Lure of the Role: The pastor's wife struggles with what she perceives are the church's expectations of her, whether real or imagined. Most of the time, they are imagined, self-driven expectations to be the "perfect" pastor's wife. We are human, so we struggle with wanting to please people, wanting them to like us, and wanting them to like our husband. The perceived role is powerful; it tempts us to maintain a certain image, rather than being authentic – revealing our weaknesses and aiming to please the Lord alone. It can also, if we let it, develop into pride: we believe the role is important, and we believe that we are to be respected and loved. Our challenge is to maintain the heart of a servant during our constant serving.

Dealing with Criticism and Cynicism: It is inevitable that the pastor and his wife will face criticism. My husband and I experienced it. Some thought the ministry did not have enough to offer them and their family, and that the congregation was too small and the list goes on. It was more physical criticism, than spiritual criticism. Some persons brought change in my life, others brought bitterness, and a few hurt me deeply. Some persons left the ministry because they believe that they were not treated justly, and some are still in ministry, but have been so wounded that they have isolated themselves, so as to never to be hurt again. Let love cover the multitude of sins.

Wrestling with the Call: Most days, pastors' wives are thankful for the call on their lives, but some days, they wish for a more "normal" existence. Sometimes we pity ourselves because of what this calling requires, or in our selfishness, we pity ourselves because our lives are centered so much on our husband's job. During my "internal wrestling," God always reminds me of the rewards of this life–rewards that many will not see. He also reminds me of Jesus' willingness to lay down His life for others, and that my calling

—a pastor's wife or not— is to give of myself for the benefit or sake of others, and for the glorification of God.

Seduction and Deception: Pastors are in a position where they are surrounded by many beautiful women. They need to ensure they make some rules and boundaries for themselves. Many pastors fall victim to infidelity and immoral living. The Bible says to watch and pray that you enter not into temptation. The spirit indeed is willing but the flesh is weak (see Matthew 26:41).

CONFLICT IN MINISTRY

"Therefore encourage one another and build up one another" (1 Thessalonians 5:11).

"PEACE IS NOT THE absence of conflict, but the presence of God no matter what the conflict" - Anonymous. "Why can't we all just get along?" Well, in short, we have all sin and come short of the glory of God. We can simply blame Adam and Eve, or we can follow Christ's example within our relationships.

All relationships, with any depth, will experience some level of conflict. Relationships we do not even acknowledge can experience conflict. It is all part of living in a fallen world. The good news is that we can look at Christ's life on earth, and see that even He was subjected to experience problems in relationships.

Having been a pastor's wife for more than twenty years, even though I have always purposely strived for peace in all relationships, I have learned that not only are some conflicts in life inevitable, but also, there can be some conflicts that are completely out of our control. Scripture tells us that peace with others is not always within our complete control: "If it is possible, *as far as it depends on you*, live at peace with everyone" (Romans 12:18).

A few years back, a conflict came to light that caused me to take a hard look at the topic of conflict, and living peacefully with other believers. This conflict was so complex, it caused me to undertake a year-long reflection on biblical peacemaking.

When faced with a fellow believer's intense anger and intolerance towards me, I sought Christ for a deeper understanding of peace, forgiveness, confession and reconciliation. In short, as a follower of Christ, I sought knowledge and wisdom about how I should respond when treated badly.

"Consider it pure joy, my sisters, whenever you face trials of many kinds, because you know that the testing of your faith develops perseverance. Perseverance must finish its work so that you may be mature and complete, not lacking anything" (James 1: 2-4).

· ·

"The Lord is close to the brokenhearted and saves those who are crushed in spirit" (Psalm 34:18). So, then, those who suffer according to God's will should commit themselves to their faithful Creator, and continue to do well (1 Peter 4:19). The one who calls you is faithful, and He will do it (1 Thess. 5:24)!

Six Important Keys to Overcoming Relationship Challenges in Ministry

B<small>E LOVING. WE HAVE</small> to love all of God's people the same as Jesus commands of us in John 13:34-35:

> A new commandment I give you that you love one another: just as I have loved you, you also are to love one another. By this all people will know that you are my disciples, if you have love for one another.

There are many characteristics of true love:

> Love bears all things, believes all things, hopes all things, and endures all things. True love never fails, does not behave itself unseemly, seeketh not her own, is not easily provoked, thinks no evil. True love never fails (1 Corinthians 13:7-8).

- Be Caring. To care for the flock is to feel concerned about them. We should have compassion for them, rather than pity.

- Be Kind: Ephesians 4:32 says, *"Be kind to one another, tenderhearted, forgiving one another, as God in Christ forgave you."*

- Trust. Have, or at the least, try to have a firm belief that the people of God are reliable, trustworthy and honest. Confident expectation and responsibility are associated with trust (Psalms 9:10).

- Honor: Every member has a place of honor in the body of Christ. Everyone deserves respect or public regards. Give honor where it is due. Do not withhold any good from the one to whom it belongs (Psalms 84:11).

- Show Respect: A level of respect should be established and given to persons in leadership, and to the saints. Even though a church member may not be in a leadership position, he or she should still be given due respect (Hebrews 13:17).

Allow THE ABOVE components to be the center of your fellowship and relationships!

How to Manage Conflict and Stay Married as a Kingdom Couple

Every relationship, even a good one has conflict. If you do not know how to deal with it, how to resolve it, or how to manage it, you can kill your relationship. There are five major areas in which your marriages may have conflict: money, sex, in-laws, children, and communication. If you both are going to pull together when conflict tries to pull you apart, you need to follow these instructions:

1. Call on God for help.

I challenge you to practice what I call "venting vertically." Many people are skilled at "venting horizontally," but venting vertically is when you go to God to talk about, or pray about the problems you face. Conflict often occurs when we expect other people to meet needs that only God can meet in our lives.

Anger is a warning light that says, "I am expecting somebody to meet my needs." When I have a need for you to be on time and you are late, or when I have a need for you to notice me and you do not, I get angry. God says, "Why don't you try talking to me about it first?" Instead of expecting your mate to meet all your needs, God wants you to look to Him.

2. Confess your part in the conflict.

Before you start attacking and blaming someone, you need to do a frank self-evaluation and ask yourself, "How much of this conflict is my fault?" When you are wrong, admit it, and when you're right, shut up! In Mathew 7:3-5 Jesus said, "*And why worry about a speck in your friend's eye when you have a log in your own? How can you think of saying to your friend, 'Let me help you get rid of that speck in your eye,' when you can't see past the log in your own eye? Hypocrite! First get rid of the log in your own eye; then you will see well enough to deal with the speck in your friend's eye.*"

Marriage is a lifelong process of overcoming your differences. Each of us has an infinite capacity for self-deception, but the fact is, it is not incompatibility- it is selfishness and an unwillingness to change.

3. Face the conflict.

Conflict does not resolve itself. It must be dealt with intentionally and expediently. Conflict gets worse when you leave it alone. Hearts grow hardened, positions get solidified, and bridges get broken beyond repair. Therefore, you have to intentionally deal with the conflict as soon as possible. The Bible is very specific about this. In Matthew 5:23-24, Jesus says:

If you enter your place of worship and you are about to make an offering, and you suddenly remember a grudge a friend has against you, abandon your offering, leave immediately, go to this friend and make things right. Then and only then, come back and work things out with God.

It is impossible to worship with bitterness in your heart and unresolved conflict with others. Postponed conflict only gets worse. **In the midst of conflict, concentrate on reconciliation, not resolution;** there is a very important difference. Reconciliation means to re-establish the relationship; resolution means to resolve every issue by coming into agreement on everything.

You will discover there are some things you and your husband are never going to agree on. It does not matter if you both love the Lord, and are passionately in love with one another. There are some things you are never going to agree on, simply because God has wired us differently. You are not going to agree with everything your mate believes or thinks, but you can disagree without being disrespectful. That is called wisdom. It is more rewarding to resolve a conflict, than it is to dissolve a relationship.

Sometimes you may need to seek professional help, and that is okay. In fact, talking to a counselor is a healthy, mature and positive choice to make, and of course, you always need to talk to God.

Many marriage conflicts would be solved overnight, if both the husband and the wife would kneel before Jesus Christ and say, "We humble ourselves, and we humbly ask you to make this thing work. We submit our egos to you and our hurts to you. Jesus Christ, do what only you can do; fix it please."

ACKNOWLEDGING AND COMMUNICATING THE ANGER YOU FEEL

THE FIRST STEP IN the process of forgiveness involves expressing your anger, and having it acknowledged. It is important to express how you are feeling. If you do not express your true feelings, they are likely to resurface, thus making forgiveness difficult to do.

Expressing your feelings, however, does not involve attacking a partner. Even though your partner has betrayed your trust or offended you in some other way, it is important to focus on how you feel, and not what your partner has done. Explain how hurt, angry and disappointed you feel, but do not bring up how disrespectful or inconsiderate your partner has been. By focusing on your feelings, rather than assigning blame, your partner is more likely to hear you out.

Expressing your feelings is only one part of the equation. Expressing your feelings is most useful when your partner acknowledges your pain. Your partner needs to validate your feelings and take ownership for what went wrong. For forgiveness to happen, your partner needs to agree with your point of view, and offer an apology. It helps to hear, "I have hurt you. I was wrong. I am sorry" (Hebrews 12:15).

This is not the time for your partner to make excuses or offer explanations. Offering excuses will only minimize your pain, and comes across as being insincere. If a partner starts to offer excuses, ask her or him to stop. Tell him that you need to feel understood before you can move on. Be direct about what you need. If you ask your partner, "How could you do this to me?" ideally, you should hear him say, "I am sorry. I put my needs ahead of what was best for our relationship."

Forgiveness happens when you can see the situation from your partner's point of view, and reflect on the incident in light of the *entire* context of your relationship. Forgiveness works when you see that your partner is a good person at heart, even though your partner is a person who just happened to make a hurtful mistake. If you personalize the problem, that is, if you view your *partner* in a negative light, rather than viewing their *actions* negatively, forgiveness will be hard to come by.

It helps to keep in mind that everyone makes mistakes. No one is perfect. Caring and loving people do very hurtful things sometimes. The more you can view what happened as an isolated incident, the easier it will be for you to forgive. Genuine forgiveness keeps relationships healthy and strong.

THE POWER OF FORGIVENESS

ALL RELATIONSHIPS FACE THEIR difficulties. At some point or another, a spouse or partner is going to betray your trust. It is how you deal with acts of betrayal that matters the most. Being able to forgive a partner for his or her transgressions is the key to a successful relationship.

How does forgiveness work? Forgiveness involves letting go of negative feelings towards a partner's misdeeds or misconduct: not seeking revenge, not holding a grudge, but viewing your partner in a positive light. Not being able to forgive a spouse creates distance; distance leads to feelings of anger and isolation, and it can have a negative impact on your health.

How exactly do you forgive a partner when they have done you wrong?

My Overcoming Testimony

I can recall a short season in my life where the enemy showed up in our marriage. I was very angry for a few days; my husband said he never saw that side of me. I felt betrayed, like someone had invaded my space and our privacy. I expressed my true feelings to my husband about how hurt I was, and what we needed to do for healing to take place. Prayer and quiet time before the Lord healed my body, my mind and my soul (Colossians 3:13-15).

My husband was surprised by how I handled the offence, continuing to be a godly wife, covering and protecting the anointing in him, while allowing the Lord to minister to him. We did not allow the matter to linger long. I showed my husband how the enemy was at work, and urgent steps were taken to bring closure to the situation. My husband was willing to ask for forgiveness. The Lord brought my heart to a place of humility, and then healing was able to take place.

> "And be ye kind one to another, tenderhearted, forgiving one another, even as God, for Christ sake, hath forgiven you" (Ephesians 4:32; Matthew 11:28-30).

The ABCD's of Being a Pastor's Wife

A – ATTITUDE: What is your true attitude toward the things of God? Do you follow His wisdom or are you more inclined to the wisdom of the world? A bad attitude is like a flat tire, you cannot go anywhere until you fix it.

Don't hang with negative people. They will pull you down with them. Instead invite them into your light and together you will both shine strong.

Abraham demonstrated the right attitude through his obedience to the Lord (Exodus 2:24).

B – BEHAVIOUR: It's the outward display of a person's attitude. If a person's attitude is negative and it is not quickly addressed, soon negative behavior will follow.

Behavior is everything. We live in a culture that is blind to betrayal and intolerant of emotional pain. This can be understood by the manner in which you behave.

Boaz demonstrated the right behavior in his submission to the Lord (Ruth 2:1-17).

C – COMMUNICATION: Communication with God should be the topmost priority in your life. Your prayer time should be like a "water's edge" quiet moments, consistent, always meditating upon His word. Paul taught young Timothy, "*study to show thyself approval unto God*" (2 Tim. 2:15) Communication is also defined as a process by which information is exchanged between individuals. The character of Christ needs to be formed in us, and spiritual maturity develops over a period of time in our lives. There are times when we need to be slow to speak and quick to listen, submitting ourselves so we can receive wisdom and instruction from the Lord.

Caleb demonstrated proper and effective communication (Numbers 10:11).

D – DISCIPLINE: Discipline means to be consistent in exercising control or being restraint in challenging times, always having self-control, a forgiving spirit and being sustained in the things of the Lord. Godly discipline is beauty to behold. You are God's representative in the earth.

David brought the victory by maintaining a relationship with the Lord (2 Sam 5:5).

Twenty Guiding Rules to Share with Your Husband

1. Never have a fleshly, close relationship with your spiritual daughter.

2. Never get emotionally attached to any female member.

3. Never post pictures of you and a spiritual daughter on a consistent basis.

4. Always bear in mind that the lady who cheaply offers herself to you, will cheaply fight you tomorrow.

5. Never take advantage of any sheep (lady) who calls you "my pastor," please, I beg you.

6. Never give financial assistance to any lady without the consent of your wife or any other third party.

7. Never pray for ladies in private places alone; ensure people are around.

8. Never allow your heart to lust after any lady. Guard your heart with all diligence.

9. Do not eat from ladies who consistently give you cooked food in the name of "he is my pastor." Remember, food is another way to a man's heart.

10. Preach against sexual immorality, and be a doer of what you preach.

11. Remind and encourage women and men to dress appropriately/respectfully for church, and also in their everyday lives outside of church.

12. If any lady is giving you signs or signals that she wants sex, openly rebuke her.

13. Never start or participate in any dirty or naughty discussion with any woman that will lead her on.

14. Try not to keep any secrets from your wife.

15. Make sure your wife is your best friend, and flaunt her anywhere, all the time.

16. Direct female members to your wife for counseling. If the case is sensitive, both of you can counsel together.

17. Often talk about your wife to others; it chases away, or repels negative and promiscuous women.

18. Express your love for your wife anywhere. Be affectionate towards your wife.

19. If any lady begins to come on to you, kindly share her thoughts with your wife.

20. Be kind to the females in your congregation, but you must be disciplined and consistent in keeping friendships/relationship professional and sanctified.

Personal and True Testimonials of Pastors' Wives

Pastor's Wife of Eleven Years:

My experience as a pastor's wife has been rewarding. I thank God for my training as it has prepared me to better maneuver through life's challenges. I find that we can sometimes compare our ministries to others, thinking we are not doing well. However, God has gifted us for various ministries, and we must fulfill the mandate/purpose that He has assigned to us. I have experienced loneliness, feelings of defeat, and moments of despair. At times we, as pastors' wives, may be misjudged or taken for granted, but I've found out that happens in all sectors of life. We must remember our calling, and who called us. We must respect our husbands as the pastor of the church and the priest of our home. We must raise our children in the fear of the Lord, and remain focused on our ministry. We must also handle the church members and community with integrity. I have found that when we can balance the above, we are able to live a life pleasing to God.

Pastor's Wife of Ten Years:

My experience as a pastor's wife for a decade was very challenging, but an experience I will never forget. At first, I never wanted to be a pastor's wife because of the experience I had growing up: I watched my mother suffered and cried many times because of the ill-treatment from my daddy, and also from some of the members of the church he pastored. My mom was a strong woman, and she was faced with many challenges like myself. I learned to pray more because I was taught never to let my problems weigh me down. As time went by, I experienced 'the true colors' of some church folks, which leads me to pray more without ceasing. It started off rough, but through it all, I am getting by through God's grace. I'm stronger than before in Jesus Christ.

Pastor's Wife of Thirteen Years:

It is incumbent upon us as pastors' wives to remain focused and always petitioning the throne in prayer. We must pray that God would remove self from us when dealing with membership: as a result of the situation, our emotions can easily hinder us from hearing from God.

One of the loneliest positions in life is being a pastor's wife. Loneliness comes as a result of not being able to balance our emotions. We are consumed with the day-to-day activities of church life, child-rearing, being the godly wife and more. As a result of so many things going on around us, we neglect ourselves. Everyone lays all their soiled laundry at our feet; their problems are offloaded into our memory banks. They share and dump; whereas, we are unable to share our concerns — our true inner feelings — because we don't want persons to judge us, or to look at us differently. Everyone expects us to be perfect and in place. No one, or few, are concerned about our hearts and what matters to us — a world of self-centered individuals.

Pastor's Wife of Thirteen Years:

I never wanted to be, or even imagined, that I would be a pastor's wife. It was not a role that I admired. I always saw beyond the glamour, and saw the pressure and responsibilities. I am a shy person who prefers to work behind the scenes, away from the 'spotlight.' However, I view my role as a pastor's wife as a calling from God, and I willingly accepted it. However, it was certainly a role I felt I was not ready for. There is a saying that, "God does not call those who are equipped, but He equips those whom He calls." I was a complete novice. I felt like I was making it up as I went along. I found no guidebook of instructions for a pastor's wife. Also, the unsolicited opinions that everyone so readily shared, only confused and frustrated me — there were so many. I had many downfalls. I made a lot of mistakes, but through it all, I saw God's hands guiding and directing me every step of the way. I shed a lot of tears. I felt lonely: suddenly it was like I was in a display case. The pressure from people's unrealistic expectations weighed me down. They expected me to be able to function in every role, from singing on the praise team, to ushering, to providing transportation to and from church functions.

I also felt vulnerable and helpless. I had no one to talk to. I felt isolated. To top it all off, I was held accountable for things that went wrong, and I had no voice or power in decision-making to fix anything. I threw many pity parties. There were times that I not only wanted to leave the church, but I also wanted to leave my marriage and quit the faith.

We are told that trials come to make us strong. I realize now, that I was in the fire to be refined. I felt like God had abandoned me—that maybe, I was being punished for some past mistake. I know now that God was right there with me all along. He was preparing me, equipping me. The pastor's wife is said to be the 'mother' of the church, a title I could not embrace when I first started out because I felt like a child in need of mothering myself. I now understand fully the comparison of the role of a pastor's wife to that of a mother. I can say that I have learned to love the members with a motherly love. I want to not only see them grow, but also assist in their development, and often that includes chastisement. I now constantly seek ways to better myself, so I can be able to give more to the congregation. I pray daily that God will pour into me, so I will in turn pour into them. I still make mistakes, but I use every mistake, every experience as a lesson. I still have reasons to cry sometimes, but I've learned to pray more. I know it's all a part of the process, and so I totally lean on God's promises, and fully trust that He's working everything out for my good.

Pastor's Wife of Eighteen Years:

One thing I can say about being a Pastor's wife, is that it is a calling. I know that there are some of you who have been in this role for much longer than I have, but I am certain that most of you will agree that this walk is a faith walk and a calling. It is God who has called us to walk by our husbands' side. In walking by my husband's side, some of my experiences have been good, and some have been not so good. I have had situations where a person (female) would not even say 'Happy Mother's Day' on that day, but when Father's Day comes around, the same individual sends a 'Happy Father's Day' to Pastor (my husband); there is always one. Then, there are those who do not respect their pastor's wife, and they always want to be 'up in the pastor's face,' and always 'need' to talk to him on the phone. On the other hand, I have also had some good experiences when the spiritually mature ladies of my church would support me in every endeavor. I encourage you women of God, continue to stay connected to the God who has called you by your husband's side. He will keep you, and fight your battles for you. God Bless.

Pastor's Wife of Seventeen Years:

My husband retired from pastoral ministry after seventeen years, but during my experience as a pastor's wife, I can say it was very exciting and challenging at the same time. A friendly, family orientated church made it happen for me. The outpouring of love and support, I believe outweighed the negative activity.

At times I wanted to implement, or bring ideas to the table, but it never came to any fruition. At times it was very frustrating, but I persevered. Being exposed to other pastors' wives, gave me the motivation to hold fast to the Lord because this is where I found strength, and the fortitude to hang in there to the end.

Pastor's Wife of Nine Years:

First, I would like to say that it is truly a joy and a privilege to be married to my husband, who God has called to be His manservant. I realize that he is a man first, then a servant of God. When we decided to get married after he had lost his wife, he told me that this journey in marriage is going to be a lonely one. He said, "You will not have the close connection with family and friends like you used to have." Well, I did not believe him. He said that people shy away from pastors because they think that God will reveal their life story to them, and because they believe that pastors are boring and 'too holy.' Thus, I learned very quickly, to build a very close and loving relationship with my husband.

I must say, even though we have a very good marriage, as mentioned, my husband was married before (his wife had passed away), so there are children on both sides. Having a blended family is not easy; there are many dynamics. The struggle is very real in having a blended family, but I must say that I see the hands of God working our situation out for the better. If I had to be married again, I would marry the same man all over again, despite the challenges. He is a man of character, a godly man, and a great husband. I would not trade him in for the world!

Prayer Coverings for Pastors and Their Wives

Prayer for Faithfulness

Dear Lord, your word says many things about faithfulness. I pray now for my husband, that he will continue to be faithful to you and to your church. Help him to always seek your direction for his life, and for the life of your church. I pray that he is faithful in all that he does: faithful to his commitments, faithful to his wife and family, faithful to his staff, but most of all, I pray that he is always faithful to you, faithful in what you would have him do. I thank you that he will accomplish your plans for his life. Lord, help him to be faithful to proclaiming your name in all the earth. I praise you for this time that I have to offer up my prayer for faithfulness Lord, and I ask that you grant these things in the name of Jesus Christ. Amen. (Psalm 89:1)

Prayer for Rest and Good Health

Dear Heavenly Father, I ask for your blessings upon my husband, that he might receive the rest that he needs from his long hours of ministry. Help me to remember that I can help him by offering to volunteer my time and talents to do the things that you gifted me to do. Help me to remember to let him know how much I appreciate the time and energy that he puts into each and everything he does. I pray that he is able to eat healthy, and get proper exercise, so that he can remain healthy for your work. I raise up this prayer in the name of your Son, Jesus Christ. Amen.

- Genesis 2:2 – *"And on the seventh day God ended his work which he had made."*

- Psalms 145:14-15 – *"The Lord upholds all that fall and raises up all those who are bowed down. The eyes of all wait upon thee; and thou give them their meat in due season."*

Prayer for Provision

Dear Lord, we love you and we know that your promises in the Bible are true. Please, hold my husband in the palm of your hands as he continually walks by faith, knowing that you will provide for his every need, as well as the needs of our family. Please, help him to remember what Jesus said about your generosity and loving-kindness. Help him to know that you know every hair on his head and that he is much more than any sparrow. I praise you for all that you have already done for my husband, and I pray that you will continue to bless him with everything that he needs. I pray these things in the precious name of Jesus Christ. Amen.

- Luke 12:6-7 – *"Are not five sparrows sold for two farthings, and not one of them is forgotten before God? But even the very hairs of your head are all numbered. Fear not therefore: ye are of more value than many sparrows."*

Prayer for Wisdom and Direction

Father in the name of Jesus Christ, I want to lift my husband up to you in prayer. He needs your wisdom and direction for your church. Please keep him humble, and always relying upon you to give him the perfect wisdom and direction that he needs. Help him to consider information offered by others, and also to come to you in prayer as he evaluates things. Remind him of your servant Solomon, who, when he was to become king, prayed only for your wisdom, and because of his humility, you granted more than wisdom. I pray this in Jesus Christ's name. Amen.

- *And God said unto him, because thou hast asked this thing, and hast not asked for thyself long life;*

neither hast asked riches for thyself, nor hast asked
the life of thine enemies; but hast asked for thyself,
understanding to discern judgment; behold, I have
done according to thy words: lo, I have given thee a
wise and an understanding heart; so that there was
none like thee before thee, neither after thee shall any
arise like unto thee. And I have also given thee that
which thou hast not asked, both riches, and honour:
so that there shall not be any among the kings like
unto thee all thy days (1 Kings 3:11-13).

- *Trust in the Lord with all thine heart; and lean*
  not unto thine own understanding. In all thy ways
  acknowledge him, and he shall direct thy paths. Be
  not wise in thine own eyes: fear the Lord and depart
  from evil (Proverbs 3:5-7).

Prayer for Fellowship and Good, Godly Friends

Dear Father in Heaven, I pray that you will provide
good and godly friends for my husband. Provide friend-
ships that will allow him to just be himself, and that will
allow him to be held accountable as a brother in Christ.
God, he needs time away from the ministry to enjoy the
fruits of his labour. I pray that you will provide good
friends that will be his for a lifetime, so that he may dwell

together with them in unity. I pray that he is able to talk about the things of the Lord, and that they may be able to encourage each other in remaining faithful, committed and loving men of God. I pray these things by the power of Jesus Christ. Amen.

- *Behold, how good and how pleasant it is for brethren to dwell together in unity! It is like the precious ointment upon the head, which ran down upon the beard, even Aaron's beard: that went down to the skirts of his garments; as the dew of Hermon, and as the dew that descended upon the mountains of Zion: for there the Lord commanded the blessing, even life forevermore* (Psalms 133).

Made in the USA
Monee, IL
30 March 2021

63230890R00105